Woman, Breathe

Leading Through Life, Career, and Business While Thriving in Every Season

Shevon "Shevvy" Maxwell

Shevon "Shevvy" Maxwell. © 2025

All rights reserved. No part of this book may be reproduced, stored, or transmitted by any

means- whether auditory, graphic, mechanical, or electronic- without the written permission of

both publisher and author, except in the case of brief excerpts used in critical articles and

certain other noncommercial uses permitted by copyright law. Unauthorized reproduction

of any part of this work is illegal and is punishable by law.

ISBN: 979-8-9938436-0-5-Paperback

Because of the dynamic nature of the internet, any web addresses or links contained in

this book may have changed since publication and may no longer be valid. The views

expressed in this work are solely those of the author and do not necessarily reflect the

views of the publisher, and the publisher disclaims any responsibility for them.

Woman, Breathe

Printed in the United States of America.

Cover Design: Justin Hardin, CEO of Damascus Media

Manuscript Editing: M. Ford, Copyediting & Proofreading

Printed in the United States of America

Shevon Maxwell

Visit www.womanbreathe.com/resources

For free resources to help you thrive through every season

Woman, Breathe

Dedication

This book is dedicated to my children, Miah, Micah, and Maya, who are my life and strength.

To my parents, Alvin and Jane, who are no longer here; and to my siblings and friends who have supported me throughout my life, career, and business journey.

Contents

Introduction viii

The S4 Framework xiv

Part 1: Self-Awareness: Self-Awareness & Identity - Being a Resilient Leader 1

    Chapter 1: Mindset Identity 1

Chapter 2: Managing Your Emotions- Leading with Emotional Intelligence and Self-Awareness 12

Chapter 3: The Resilient Leader Mindset 19

Part 2: Strength: Resilience & Renewal - The Resilient Leader Activation 31

Chapter 4: Effective Decision-Making: A Defining Element of Leadership 31

Chapter 5: Stress Management for Leading with Resilience 43

Part 3: Stewardship: Leadership & Influence- Practical Leadership Strategies for Building a Resilient Culture ... 58

Chapter 6: Building & Leading Resilient Teams 58

Chapter 7: Leading Through Communication and Managing Conflict 68

Chapter 8: Operating With Purpose 79

Part 4: Sustainability: Growth & Alignment - Lifestyle Strategies for Sustained Resilience 90

Chapter 9: Lifestyle Habits for Resilient Leadership 90

Chapter 10: The Power of Movement and Brain Performance 97

Chapter 11: Leading in Every Season- Self-Care as a Leadership Strategy to Lead in Any Season of Life, Career, and Business 105

Closing 110

Chapter Summary: Thriving in Every Season 112

About the Author 116

The Journey Continues 118

My commitment to resilience and thriving in every season and my hopes for you. 118

Your Next Steps 118

Access Free Resources and Digital Products: 118

Introduction

"Your time to shift and start thriving in every season is now."

Welcome to *Woman, Breathe: Leading Through Life, Career, and Business While Thriving in Every Season.*

Thank you for purchasing this book. I don't take it lightly that you chose to invest your time and trust here. My hope is that as you read, you begin to see yourself in these pages, wherever you are on your journey in life, career, or business, and the weight you've been carrying along the way.

This book is here to guide you, remind you, and assure you that no matter the season or the environment, you can reset, lead, and thrive. And if you're reading these words, I know you've reached a point where something has to change - now and not later.

You've picked up this book because you know something has to shift in the way you're leading and showing up in your life, career, and business.

Right now, you're moving so fast that slowing down feels impossible. At home, you're holding it all together while running on fumes. You catch yourself snapping at your kids

Woman, Breathe

when all they want is your attention, leaving you feeling guilty. You're snapping at your partner, close friend, and team.

The constant weight of decisions leaves your mind exhausted before the day even ends. And in your career, the weight of responsibility follows you long after you've left the office. It feels like you don't even have space to breathe before the next problem lands on your desk. And in your business, you're carrying the pressure of always having to know the answer, even when you're running on empty. You're juggling clients, deadlines, and money decisions that keep you up at night. And behind the smile, you're carrying stress and overwhelm that no one sees. The truth is, you're showing up everywhere but feeling fully present nowhere.

You see, I was you.

When I was serving in the United States Air Force, I thought I could do it all. As an ambitious woman I was always doing something. In 2010, I was a mom of one and pregnant with my second child, a wife, in graduate school, and training military instructors every six weeks. A few months after giving birth, I traveled to Virginia to buy our first home with a newborn in my arms during the summer.

But the truth? I was burnt out but didn't know it. Before moving to our next duty station during the last quarter of 2010, I landed in the emergency room mentally drained, physically exhausted, and completely out of balance. My blood pressure was high and I had no clue; my body was shutting down, and I didn't even notice because running like the Energizer Bunny (**keep going and going**) had become my normal.

That season pushed me into a vertigo episode. Intrusive thoughts I had never experienced before led to anxiety. I was scared of the woman I was becoming. I questioned whether I'd ever get back to laughing, dancing, moving my body with joy, and being *me*.

That breaking point became my turning point. It forced me to stop living on autopilot and start rebuilding with intention. Through self-awareness, strength, stewardship, and sustainability, the framework I now teach, I learned to breathe again. Movement became part of my mental and overall healing, and so did redefining what it meant to lead and live well.

From there, everything shifted and it was not an easy journey. I earned multiple promotions and was part of the top

Woman, Breathe

2 % of the Air Force's Military Enlisted Leaders. I retired from the Air Force with honors. I launched my businesses, MAC Leadership Academy, and J3M Consulting. I've helped business owners not just shift their mindset, but strengthen their operations, increase their revenue, and build businesses they can sustain.

I share this because I know what it feels like to carry everything and lose yourself in the process. And, I also know you can come back stronger mentally, emotionally, and physically because I did it.

The purpose of *Woman, Breathe™: Leading Through Life, Career, and Business While Thriving in Every Season* is simple: to give you the chance to pause, recommit to yourself, and break free from the cycle that leads to burnout, hospitalization, or worse. This is your self-leadership and wellness blueprint to start thriving in every season of life, career, and business.

I've lived this and continue to live with a thriving mindset. I used these same strategies to make myself a priority, reclaim my identity, heal from anxiety, be more present with my kids, walk through divorce after 15 years, and build relationships no matter the type of friendship without losing me or my mental readiness. These strategies helped me keep thriving in life, career as a retired Air Force Senior Master Sergeant, and now business owner.

This is not the book to skim and set aside. This is the book you finish. Because when you commit to the end, you'll have the habits, tools, and strategies you need to shift how you reset, lead, and thrive. Through the S4 Framework ™: Self-awareness, Strength, Stewardship, and Sustainability, you'll learn how to thrive in every season.

You already possess the resilience, readiness, and leadership within you. Now it's time to put it to work. Not just plan, but take action to create the shift you've been wanting.

Imagine leading without constant exhaustion, being more present with your kids, and building a business or career that fuels you, not drains you. Once you read *Woman, Breathe™: Leading Through Life, Career, and Business While Thriving in Every Season,* you will be equipped to create the shift you need to lead and thrive in every season and environment. You don't have to wait to start creating and living the life you want. You get to decide today!

Your time to shift and start thriving in every season, is now.

Woman, Breathe

Thriving in Every Season

Shevon aka Shevvy

Shevon Maxwell

The S4 Framework

Before we dive deeper into the chapters ahead, I want to share the framework that anchors this book.

The S4 Framework is a four-step method I created to help women align identity, resilience, leadership, and growth so they can thrive in every season of life, career, and business. It's built from my lived experiences: growing up with humble beginnings in South America (Guyana), moving to Newark, New Jersey 10 days before my 10th birthday, leaving home to join the Air Force at 19, leading through 22+ years of military service, and navigating the challenges of motherhood, transitions, and entrepreneurship. The S4 Framework is built upon a self-leadership and wellness blueprint that equips women to thrive personally and lead resiliently in life, career, and business.

This framework isn't a theory; it's a practical guide. Each "S" represents a building block of resilience, leadership, and wellness that you will see woven throughout this book:

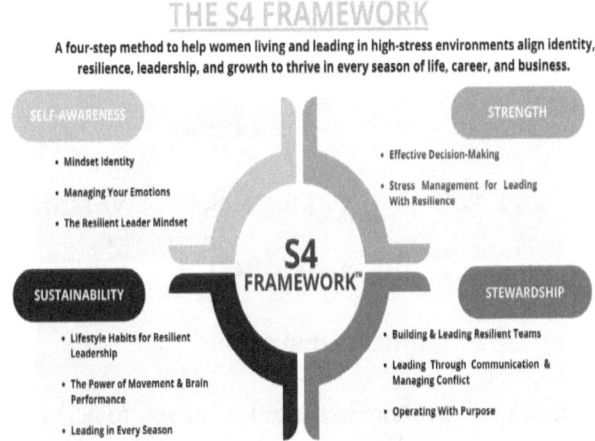

As you read, you'll notice how each chapter ties back to one or more of these pillars. The S4 Framework™ is here to give you a path not just for knowledge, but for action so you can thrive in life, career, and business.

"When you know how your brain operates as a woman, you know how to build your resilience muscles, and create a foundation of strength that will serve you before a crisis even comes."

Part 1: Self-Awareness: Self-Awareness & Identity - Being a Resilient Leader

Chapter 1: Mindset Identity

I decided to start here because I want you to understand how your brain operates as a woman leader from a neuroscience perspective. Whether you're navigating life, career, or business, you are the leader in each role. You lead with your brain and mind, so understanding how you're mentally showing up in those roles will help you navigate challenges, make decisions, manage stress, communicate effectively, set boundaries, and so much more. When you know how your brain operates as a woman, you know how to build your resilience muscles. You create a foundation of strength that will serve you before a crisis even comes. No matter the environment, you put yourself in a position to remain composed during chaos, so you can handle situations while making clear, effective decisions.

While growing up in Newark, New Jersey, I never heard about neuroscience in my community. But looking back, I now believe people in my community were aware of the principles, but the term neuroscience simply wasn't talked about. Resilience was another word I didn't hear, but it was in action all around me. I just didn't realize it was in me, too.

That changed when I began thinking seriously about starting my own business. My life experiences with anxiety pushed me to search for answers. One day, while scrolling social media, I came across a Facebook ad from Shonté Jovan Taylor, and I was instantly intrigued. Shonté Jovan Taylor (Neuroscientist), is the founder of the Optimind Institute: a consulting, coaching, research, and personal and professional development training entity designed specifically for reputable coaches, trainers, leaders, and organizations. At that time, I was a single mom to three children, 14, 9, and 8 months old, while my partner was still overseas. I was working full-time on active duty in the Air Force, enrolled in a doctoral program, and navigating life during the COVID-19 pandemic.

The more I learned from Shonté, the more fascinated I became with understanding this field of neuroscience. I realized that learning about the neuroscience of leadership, emotions, and the "CEO brain" would help me as a mom, military career woman, and business owner, serving my family, my military community, and my future clients.

By studying and applying what I learned, I began to respond differently and more effectively, especially under stress. I learned how to tap into my higher brain. I started to see things and people differently. I became more resilient because I understood what was happening in my brain during high-pressure moments. Parenting, leading, running operations, or building a business no longer had to mean being overwhelmed.

And this is what I want for you, too: to understand the power of your brain's resilience. When you know how to regulate your response, you don't let the chaos of life, career, or business make you feel like you're losing control. Instead, you step fully into being a resilient leader, one who embraces challenges with confidence because she knows how to be mentally strong.

Defining Resilience and Its Role in Leadership

What is resilience? According to the American Psychological Association (APA), resilience is *"the process and outcome of successfully adapting to difficult or challenging life experiences, especially through mental, emotional, and behavioral flexibility and adjustment to external and internal demands."*

That's the formal definition. But how do *you* define resilience? For me, it's simple: resilience is the ability to manage the mental noise in my head so that I can keep moving forward and thrive in any environment, no matter what challenges come my way.

As you'll see throughout this book, I've had life, career, and business experiences that could have broken me, moments where fear consumed me, and where the weight felt too heavy. But I had a choice: let fear control my life or take control of it myself. I chose resilience. I chose to lean into my self-talk strategies, regulate my emotions, and keep moving forward even when I wanted to stop.

As a leader, you're currently facing challenges or will face challenges in your role. And as a woman leader, the truth is, your plate is already full. But here's the danger: if you don't pay attention, that plate gets so heavy it shatters into pieces, leaving you spiraling mentally, emotionally, and physically. That spiral doesn't just affect you, it affects your family, your team, your business, and your ability to show up whole.

That's why resilience matters. It's not just about surviving tough moments; it's about leading well *through* them. It's about shifting from holding a title of "leader" to owning the identity of a **resilient woman leader:** someone who knows how to navigate life, career, and business without losing herself in the process.

Understanding the Woman's Brain for Building Resilience

Understanding how your brain functions differently from men's helps you to understand who you are, how you operate, and how you respond to situations.

Woman, Breathe

As women, our brains are naturally wired in ways that allow us to connect dots faster, feel emotions deeply, and notice details that others may miss. That's why you can be in a meeting or on the phone, and still remember what your child asked you for earlier or the details your team has shared. It's how you juggle life, career, and business, because your brain is designed to process a lot at once.

Think of your brain like a busy airport. Planes (thoughts) are constantly landing and taking off. Some are big international flights (major decisions), while others are short connections (daily tasks). When everything is running smoothly, air traffic control (your resilience) directs each plane where it needs to go. But when there's too much traffic, storms, or delays, the airport gets backed up, and that's when you feel overwhelmed, stressed, and mentally drained.

Building resilience is about training your brain to be a steady air traffic controller. Instead of letting stress and overthinking cause chaos, you create space, slow down the reaction, and guide each thought where it belongs. You begin to use your emotions as information, not as chains that hold you back.

Your brain is powerful. And when you understand how it works, you give yourself permission to lead with more confidence, calm, and strength in every area of your life.

Identity: Signs It's Time to Shift

You're currently experiencing things in your life, and you know they feel overwhelming, but you're ignoring the signs. Becoming the resilient woman starts with you deciding, so continuing to ignore the signs will not be good for your overall well-being. It wasn't good for *my* mental health and overall well-being because **I chose to ignore the signs.**

I didn't pay attention to the signs even though my body was giving me all the signals, the same ones that may be coming up for you right now as a woman leader, and a business owner. The inability to focus. The burning sensations in your body, ears, back, feet, neck. The dizziness and lightheadedness. The constant fidgeting. Not being fully present to the little things, especially if you're a parent.

I was you! I was overwhelmed. I was exhausted. I was drained and felt the weight of being the mom, the wife at the time, the military member, the graduate student… and still I kept going. **I kept going!**

You may be putting your career or business over everything else. Your time is running away from you, and your time management is out of whack. Maybe you're experiencing mood swings, ineffective communication, or indecisiveness because the weight of doing it all is just too heavy. I've been there too. I ignored it all until my body finally forced me to stop. Then came vertigo, the ER, and years of dealing with anxiety because I wouldn't acknowledge the signs.

These signs are common, especially for us as women, because we keep showing up for our kids, our partners, our husbands, our jobs, our businesses, while leaving ourselves behind. But ignoring the signs leads to burnout, over and over again.

The key is this: the shift begins when you choose to identify and acknowledge the signs. When you do, you begin stepping into the flow of becoming the resilient woman leader, the one who has a big vision, who is building her business to thrive, who is elevating in her career without losing herself.

For me, the shift came after serving 22-plus years in the United States Air Force. I had lost myself for a moment, but today I am deliberate about managing my mental, physical, and emotional well-being as I build my business. Because without it, I can't live the life I've worked hard for. I had to ask myself: *What's actually happening in my brain when stress takes over?* That's where the neuroscience of resilience came in, and it changed everything.

How to Develop the Mindset Identity to Help You Thrive in Every Season

Here are three steps to developing your mindset identity so you can lead and operate in any environment.

Shevon Maxwell

Step 1: Notice your mental alerts
Pay attention to the thoughts running through your head, because they're driving how you lead, the energy you carry, and the decisions you make. Ask yourself: *What am I thinking right now? Is it helping me, or is it keeping me stuck in survival mode?* You'll know you're in survival mode when your body feels tense, you're frustrated, angry, crying, or ready to attack. Catch those alerts. Don't let them run the show. The quicker you catch them, the quicker you can shift.

Step 2: Decide your resilience response
When challenges come, I want you to decide in advance how you're going to show up. This is how you build that resilience muscle so you don't spiral out when people test you, when conflict hits, or when things feel uncertain. Instead of reacting too quickly, sending that text, firing off that email, or walking into someone's office ready to go off, you pause. You breathe. You choose your response. That one decision can shift the entire situation.

Step 3: Name your resilience wins
Think back on situations where you could've gone off, but you didn't. That's a resilience win. Maybe you didn't send that email right away. Maybe you held your tongue when your kids pushed you. Maybe you didn't cut your partner off mid-sentence. Or maybe somebody came at you sideways on purpose, but you chose not to react. Those are all wins. Don't brush them off. Call them

out. The more you name those wins, the more you train yourself to bounce back stronger the next time life comes at you.

Storytime: Building My Resilience Muscle During Tough Times- The Loss of a Parent

It was around 7:30 in the morning on November, 2018, and I was in my office at Royal Air Force Mildenhall in the United Kingdom, getting ready to start my day, checking emails, responding to messages, just settling in. Then my personal phone rang. It was my dad.

When I answered, I heard him yell, "She's gone, she's gone, my daughter, she's gone!" My heart sank. I said, "What, Alvin? What do you mean?" (Yes, I called my dad by his first name, it's part of my Guyanese culture.) And then it hit me. He was telling me my mother had passed away.

In that moment, I closed my office door and cried. I cried as my dad tried to find the words, and then I pulled myself together long enough to ask if my siblings knew. He said no, he couldn't find the strength to call anyone else. So, I did what came naturally to me. I stepped into leadership mode. I picked up the phone and started calling my siblings one by one, notifying them of the news. Even though I was the fourth child out of nine, I was the one who took the lead. That's who I am. That's what the Air Force trained in me.

And maybe you're the same, the one who gets things done even in the hardest moments.

But here's the truth: I was broken inside. I was holding it together for everyone else while my own world felt like it was crashing down. I cried when I told my kids about their grandmother, and I cried again at home when I was finally alone. But even through the tears, I leaned into resilience.

What got me through that moment was my mindset. I let myself grieve, but I didn't let the grief take me under. I tapped into my resilience muscle; the same one I'd been building through every challenge before this. It allowed me to keep moving, to make the calls, to arrange the funeral, and to carry my family through something none of us were prepared for.

Losing my mom was one of the hardest moments of my life. And it shifted everything: how I showed up as a mom, as a leader, as a woman. But it also reminded me of this truth: resilience isn't optional. Life will hand you seasons that break your heart and test your strength. What matters is how you respond, and how you hold on to yourself in the process.

Chapter 1 Reflective Activity: Developing Your Mindset Identity

Focus on you so you can thrive in life, career, and business.

What three habits, choices, or patterns are you holding onto right now that keep you in burnout, create setbacks, or cause you to repeat old struggles? Write them down honestly.

What is one new action you can start today that will bring more ease into your life, career, or business? Define exactly how you'll take the first step.

What is one thing you can stop doing today that fuels your burnout or drains your energy? **How will that impact your current state?**

When you control your thoughts, you control your life. Resilience begins with mindset, and it's the key to building a life, career, and business that is both sustainable and joyful.

But mindset alone isn't enough. The real test comes when emotions hit hard. In the next chapter, we'll walk through how to manage your emotions so you don't just survive the chaos, but actually lead yourself through it with clarity and strength.

"You cannot control every situation, but you can control how you respond."

Chapter 2: Managing Your Emotions- Leading with Emotional Intelligence and Self-Awareness

Leading Emotionally Well

When it comes to leading emotionally well, it is your responsibility as a woman leader to manage your emotions through difficult times, challenges, frustrations, and chaos in every environment. When you lead emotionally well, you create a more fulfilled life, reduce stress, and build an environment that is safe for you and others, a space people want to be part of.

Leading emotionally well is about understanding and managing your emotions. When people do things that might make you yell, cry, or lose your temper, you choose instead to respond with emotional regulation, mindfulness, and resilience in your life, career, or business. Owning your emotions allows you to communicate effectively without attacking or talking down to others.

Leading emotionally well means staying in character when people or situations try to push you out of it. But when you're under stress from family, career, and business demands, it can feel overwhelming and cause you to lose yourself in the process. That's why understanding and regulating your emotions will serve you well, helping you thrive in every area of your life, career, and business while building your emotional and mental resilience muscles.

Strategies to Cultivate More Self-Awareness
As a woman leader, you want to cultivate strategies that help you become more self-aware to lead better in your life, career, and business. *Travis Bradberry & Jean Greaves: EMOTIONAL INTELLIGENCE 2.0* breaks down the four pillars of emotional intelligence:

- Self-awareness
- Self-management
- Social awareness
- Relationship management

Your willingness to master these four pillars will strengthen your resilience and allow you to operate with high emotional intelligence. In this chapter, I focus on the two core pillars that were essential to me: **self-awareness** and **self-management**.

Self-awareness is about regulating yourself when life feels like it's about to knock you down. It's knowing when you're exhausted so you don't snap at your kids, partner, coworkers, or boss. It's noticing your emotions and reactions in real time so you can respond with clarity.

Being self-aware means recognizing habits you already know about yourself. Maybe you're impatient. Maybe you interrupt others mid-sentence (I've been guilty of this myself), but you work on regulating your emotions by waiting until they finish speaking. Sometimes family or colleagues call you out on habits you haven't corrected yet; that's your opportunity to grow. Becoming aware of yourself determines how well you self-manage your emotions.

Chapter 2 Self-Awareness Activity
What habits show up daily that affect your emotional, mental, and physical well-being?
1. Draw a large circle and divide it into three sections.
2. Label each section: Emotional, Mental, Physical.
3. List the habits you're aware of, including the ones others have pointed out to you.
4. Take three minutes for each section to reflect.

Self-Management
Self-management is intentionally addressing the habits you identified in self-awareness. How are these habits affecting your life and work performance? How will you correct them? How will you create time for what serves your well-being, your mental health, and your ability to show up fully?

This is where self-care and resilience-building practices matter. When you incorporate recovery habits, you strengthen your mental resilience and grow as a leader.

Tools for Managing Emotions Under Pressure
There will be many times when people test you in the workplace, in leadership, and even in personal relationships. As a woman leader, you must understand that people will sometimes act out of insecurity, envy, or bias. Some may be threatened by your position, your life, or your business. Others simply won't like you.

Here are three strategies to manage your emotions when you face negativity, pressure, or stress:

1. **Step away.** Go for a walk to reset your nervous system and lower stress. Movement reduces adrenaline, calms your heart rate, and clears your mind.

2. **Take a deep breath.** Slow, intentional breathing calms your nerves, lowers your heart rate, and shifts your brain from fear to clarity.

3. **Close your mouth.** Give your brain time to process before responding. This can be hard in the moment, but closing your mouth prevents regret and allows you to respond with strength instead of impulse.

When life is happening, remind yourself that you can regulate your emotions. Becoming a resilient woman leader means going back to self-awareness, self-management, and building habits that keep you grounded. Choosing not to lose control allows you to release stress, walk away from relationships or environments that no longer serve you, and navigate life, career, and business without losing yourself.

Storytime: The Day I Let My Emotions Lead
I was twenty, going on twenty-one, and had been in the military for about two years at Minot Air Force Base in North Dakota. I was preparing for a career development test to receive my five-level upgrade, which is required for promotion. Education was always important to me, and the Air Force required these tests to progress in rank and leadership responsibilities.

In my squadron, airmen usually received the day off before the test and the day of the test. I received the day off before, but not the day of. When I learned another airman, a white female, did not have to return to work while I did, I lost control. I was angry, yelling on the phone to leadership, demanding to know why I had to return when she did not. Looking back, I can see the favoritism that fueled my reaction, but in that moment, I wasn't emotionally regulated.

Too often, women are labeled as "crazy" or "irrational" when we express frustration. In that moment, my best friend calmed me down and reminded me it wasn't worth it. I'm grateful she did, because my reaction could have derailed my career. Instead, I went on to serve twenty-two years and retired as a Senior Master Sergeant.

That experience taught me how quickly emotions can damage credibility. It reminded me that as women leaders, we must learn to reset ourselves before emotions cut short the opportunities we've worked so hard for.

Lessons Learned
- Emotional regulation is the foundation of leadership.
- Self-awareness helps you notice your triggers before they control you.

- Self-management allows you to correct behaviors that no longer serve you.

- Responding with regulation builds trust and credibility; reacting from anger creates setbacks.

- Resetting yourself is key to protecting your future.

Chapter 2 Reflective Activity: Checking your emotions

Identify a recent situation where you did not respond emotionally well in your life, career, or business:

- What was the core issue that triggered your response?

- What emotions came up (thoughts and feelings)?

- What behaviors showed up?

- What could you have done differently?

- What will you do next time?

You cannot control every situation, but you can control how you respond. Your emotional responses directly impact how others see you and how you see yourself. When you choose regulation over reaction, you create resilience, protect your credibility, and build a leadership style that thrives in every season of life, career, and business.

> *"Resilience is not the absence of fear; it's the decision to face fear differently."*

Chapter 3: The Resilient Leader Mindset

Breaking Down the Neuroscience of Mindset and Belief
Tapping into our growth mindset is essential for our mental well-being. I know from experience why a fixed mindset keeps you stuck. There was a portion of my life when my mindset was in the fixed zone, fueled by the fear I generated with my own thoughts. That fear, combined with extreme burnout, led to vertigo.

I want you to understand the power of operating in a growth mindset versus a fixed mindset, which was introduced by Carol S. Dweck, Ph.D., in her book *Mindset: The New Psychology of Success: How We Can Learn to Fulfill Our Potential* (2016). In her book, Carol noted, "People in a growth mindset don't just seek challenge, they thrive on it." (p. 21, *Stretching*). This is me. If I'm not challenged, I get bored and start to procrastinate. Maybe you're the same, or maybe you're not. At the end of the day it's up to me, and it's up to you, to tap into building a resilient mindset, and that begins with expanding your growth mindset.

In simple terms, a fixed mindset is when you're fixated on a situation, a problem, what you don't have, or what isn't working in your life, business, or career. On the opposite side, operating in a growth mindset is about looking at possibilities and opportunities, taking stock of your circumstances, and knowing that it's not the end. You look at challenges differently, and you choose to move forward instead of staying stuck in a fixed mindset.

When you stay in a fixed mindset, it can lead to emotional and physical damage to the body and mind because you keep yourself in a cycle where you see the glass half empty instead of half full. Building a resilient, growth mindset takes courage, it takes time, and it takes belief.

Reflection Story

During my challenges with parenting, going through a divorce, living with anxiety, my military career, launching a business, and the loss of my mother, I had to make sure I didn't allow doubts, fears, and constant mental questioning to keep me stuck in a fixed mindset. Because I chose to shift my thoughts and belief system, I was able to focus on the good things that were happening for me so I didn't lose myself.

Fighting through the mental noise helps you move into a growth mindset so you don't lose yourself in the chaos of life, career, or business. When I look back at my life's situations and all the things I've overcome, serving on active duty in the military, being a mom to three, my time as a wife and partner, and building a business, I've always tried my best to look at what's next, even when I allowed myself a mini pity party.

I never let my situation or circumstances keep me down for long. In my mind, I refused to stay in a fixed place where I kept asking, *Why isn't this working for me? Why aren't things going my way?* Yes, I asked those questions sometimes, but I didn't allow myself to stay there. Instead, I shifted my mindset to look at what wasn't working and asked, *What can I do about it?*

This is critical when you're developing a resilient mindset during life's challenges. When you catch yourself focusing on the fixed mindset, what isn't going right in your life, your business, or your career, and your thoughts start pulling you down into your lower brain, I want you to pivot. Ask yourself instead:

- What is going right in my life?

- What is going right in my career?
- What is going right in my business?

Because at the end of the day, your self-talk is what moves you and keeps you in the growth mindset, which directly impacts your resilience. If your self-talk is negative, you'll spend more time stuck in a fixed mindset. But as a resilient woman leader, you can choose to operate in a growth mindset no matter the circumstance, the situation, or the environment.

When you tap into your growth mindset, you truly step into being that resilient woman. You start to see things differently. You make decisions differently. You see yourself differently. You begin to see yourself as a woman who can overcome anything and that is the strength of building a resilient growth mindset.

So always take time to breathe and then choose the mindset that will move you forward.

Overcoming Setbacks and Failures with Resilience
Overcoming failures with resilience is all about not allowing the things that happen in life, career, or business to derail you from moving forward. It comes down to how you see

yourself, how you think about yourself, and the actions you choose to take. As you continue to build and develop as a woman leader, you're going to experience setbacks. You're going to experience failures. You will face unexpected situations that are completely out of your control.

I've had setbacks in my military career where coworkers tried to portray me in a negative light, or taint my character in front of my team and leadership because they felt threatened by how I showed up. But I still showed up confidently. I led confidently. I used my voice confidently. I connected confidently. I walked into rooms confidently. That experience did not define how I showed up or how I led in my role.

When it comes to you, you cannot let other people, your circumstances, or your life experiences define who you are or how you show up as a leader in your life, career, or business. To overcome failure and setbacks and step into being a resilient and bold woman leader, you have to shift your mindset into belief and growth. When you focus only on what's not working, you activate your fear brain. When that happens, your brain is five times more likely to keep focusing on fear, which keeps you mentally in the past, stuck in your current situation, and prevents you from showing up fully as the woman you want to be in your life, career, and business.

When you fail to show up fully, you create the narrative for others to see you as a leader who is not capable or competent. But when you shift into a growth mindset, you open yourself to possibilities. You expand your ability to handle challenges and tough situations. You learn to see failures as opportunities. You begin to view setbacks as moments for growth. As you step more fully into your leadership role, trust yourself to be that resilient woman leader who is in control mentally, emotionally, and physically. Trust yourself to handle situations and setbacks so you can keep living, keep leading, and keep moving forward as the resilient, strong, audacious, and bold leader you were created to be.

Storytime: Turning Fear into Fuel
You have to look at fear and turn it into fuel so you can leave the mental dark place and create a new life without being trapped in the fear brain. During my time in the military, the stress and demands of managing a home, raising two kids under five, and being a wife led me to be transported by ambulance to the emergency room. That moment marked the

beginning of my struggle with anxiety. My life shifted completely. I became a different person because of the intrusive negative thoughts that consumed my mind.

I had unhealthy thoughts, especially around the safety and well-being of my children. The fear that came with those thoughts stopped me from truly living and enjoying life. I only wanted to go to work, come home, cook for my kids, and go to sleep, just to shut my mind off.

But I had to make a choice. I had to choose not to allow fear to control me. I had to use my anxiety as fuel and courage to step into the woman I knew I was: the woman who loves to have fun, who is driven, who is a visionary, who loves life, and who loves her children.

Maybe right now you're in a place where you feel like a failure, or you think you should be further along. This is your reminder: you will get through this. And it starts with choosing your mindset and seeing yourself differently. For me, that shift began with small strategies. I talked to myself. I even sang the artist Nelly's song, "It's all in my head" (just that one part)! Self-talk became part of my healing, part of becoming a resilient woman leader.

I journaled every day for a long time because I had to rewire my brain. My thoughts had become too dark for my mental well-being and for the safety of my two young children. At first, my journaling fed my fear brain because I focused on unhealthy thoughts. But over time, I began to shift. I started journaling healthy thoughts: "I am grateful for my life. I am not crazy. It's all in my head."

Journaling allowed me to overcome fear little by little. It gave me the strength to be more present, to lead better, to be a better parent, to be a better wife at the time, and to be better to myself. As you continue to grow into the resilient woman you're called to be, I want you to see your failures and setbacks as opportunities to move forward. Don't allow your fear brain to take control. Choose to lead your life, career, and business with resilience.

Lessons Learned
- Setbacks and failures don't define you; they reveal opportunities for growth.
- A fixed mindset keeps you stuck in fear; a growth mindset opens new possibilities.
- When you focus on what's not working, you activate your fear brain. Shift your self-talk to move forward.

- Confidence isn't about being perfect; it's about choosing to show up fully, even when others try to tear you down.

- Resilience grows when you turn fear into fuel and use challenges to strengthen your belief system.

- Daily habits like journaling and self-talk can rewire your mind, helping you step out of fear and into resilience.

Chapter 3 Activity: Self-Talk Mind Mapping
Take this opportunity to create a mind map of your thoughts.

1. Draw a circle and divide it down the middle. Label one side *Fixed Mindset* and the other *Growth Mindset*.

2. List all of your current thoughts under each column.

3. Write down five growth affirmations or quotes you can look at daily to anchor yourself in a growth mindset.

Strategies for Building a Resilient Mindset
1. Speak it daily: Use affirmations to reinforce a growth mindset
What you say to yourself daily is cemented into your

neurons, creating connections and sending messages throughout your mind. Positive affirmations reinforce and strengthen your memory bank, which stores your thoughts and experiences.

2. Practice gratitude: Write 10 things you're grateful for each day for 30 days

You feed your mind every day with your thoughts and your words. A daily gratitude exercise for 30 days will shift how you think and see yourself. It helps you transition from a fixed mindset to an abundance mindset. When I was experiencing challenges with anxiety, I started journaling my thoughts. At first, those thoughts were dark and didn't serve me. However, when I started keeping a daily gratitude journal, I began to rewire my brain.

3. Release the cycle of doubt: Give yourself 5, 10, or 15 minutes to process setbacks, then move forward

Doubt will keep you planted when you need to move. When you feel stuck, give yourself grace but also set a limit, no more than 15 minutes to process the emotions. Then, make the choice not to let doubt lead you.

Client testimony: Keshawn was looking for clarity and participated in my one hour intensive and she left with clarity, mindset shift and offer elevation to generate more revenue in her business.

> " Shevvy brings a wealth of knowledge, experience, and genuine support to every interaction. After one conversation with her, I walked away with sharpened clarity about my value as a coach and business offerings that inspired immediate action. Her commitment to help leaders lead with ease is unmistakable and her gift of discernment is unmatched. I'm thankful to be in her network!

Keshawn Ridgel Hughes, M.S.
Neurocoach | Marketing Consultant| Instructor

Resilience is not the absence of fear; it's the decision to face fear differently. When you shift into a growth mindset, you don't just survive; you thrive. You begin to see yourself as capable of overcoming anything. You lead with courage, clarity, and resilience in life, career, and business.

Take a breath, reset your mind, and remember you are stronger than your fear.

Action Assignment: Take this further by getting your 7-Day Mindset and Wealth Building Affirmation Cards. Use them daily to strengthen your growth and wealth mindset. And continue building resilience as a leader. Visit www.womanbreathe.com to download your 7-Day Mindset and Wealth Building Affirmation Cards.

"If I didn't choose me, I would lose me."

Part 2: Strength: Resilience & Renewal - The Resilient Leader Activation

Chapter 4: Effective Decision-Making: A Defining Element of Leadership

Becoming a resilient leader is a decision you must choose as you navigate the challenges and uncertainties of life, career, and business. Being a resilient leader starts with self-control. It takes belief, consistent action, and dedication to show up as a woman leader, and that begins with deciding.

How you make decisions impacts the next action and the next outcome. How you respond to those actions and outcomes won't always lead to the results you want. That's why going back to your emotional intelligence, specifically the two quadrants of self-awareness and self-management, will determine how you transition to the next phase of your situation.

As you make decisions as a woman leader, your competence will be tested. But your life, career, and business experiences all add to your competence level. You already have the experience and ability to make effective decisions in high-stress situations and environments.

When you trust yourself and operate at your best, you are able to:

- Regulate your emotions
- Handle challenges
- Plan for the future
- Draw on the willpower to move forward
- Self-reflect
- Identify risks with mental clarity

When you're not stressed or burned out, you're able to make the best decisions in the moment. That's because you're engaging your prefrontal cortex, the part of your brain that regulates your responses and leads the rest of your brain.

Your prefrontal cortex ensures that all parts of your brain work together effectively. But when you're under extreme stress, your brain shifts into survival mode. In that state, your ability to make competent decisions is compromised, impacting how you lead yourself, your team, your business, and your life.

When you are under chronic stress, your brain can't make effective and competent decisions. Brain science shows that your ability to process, think clearly and respond appropriately decreases significantly during periods of extreme stress.

According to Dr. Shonte' Jovan Taylor, Neuroscientist (n.d), founder of the Optimind, Institute, Think of your hippocampus as your brain's "memory bank." It's part of your brain that transfers short-term memories into long-term ones which is located in your emotional brain that is next to your amygdala. That's the area that is tied to our emotions, life fear, anxiety, fear, and stress. And when you're under chronic stress, your memory bank becomes overloaded and starts to wear down, which can impact how you remember, react, and make decisions.

You're not able to focus. You're not able to have the clarity needed to make sound decisions, to hear all the facts, or to gather all the information. You're not able to communicate effectively because the stress you're under prevents you from articulating yourself clearly.

I know this from lived experience. I served 22-plus years in the United States Air Force. I'm a mom of three. I've gone through a divorce. I've lost my mom. I've transitioned out of the military. I've ended a seven-year relationship. The stress that came with all of that affected my decision-making because I didn't always have the mental clarity I needed to show up as the effective leader I know I am.

When you're under Distress (stress), your heart rate increases. Mental fatigue increases. Your ability to sleep decreases. Your ability to reset yourself disappears. As you navigate your life, career, and business, the continuous stress you put on yourself will eventually impact you mentally, emotionally, and physically.

Some stress is good when you're achieving tangible goals. We actually have two types of stress: **eustress** and **distress.**

- Eustress (Positive stress) pushes you forward. It strengthens your resilience, helps you overcome obstacles, and fuels you to move forward. It's that adrenaline rush that gives your mind energy to keep going, like when you finish school, get a promotion, or launch a business.

- Distress, on the other hand, begins to deteriorate your mental capacity. It starts breaking down the neurons and healthy brain connections you need to show up as the woman leader in all areas of your life.

When you are under extreme stress, your memory bank takes the hit. You start forgetting things. You can't remember where you left your keys. You can't remember if you made a decision on something. You can't even remember what you had for lunch. All of these are signs that you're under extreme stress, and that something negative is about to happen if you don't address it.

When you're operating under extreme stress, you're also not able to make the best decisions. You increase risk not only for yourself, but also for your family, career, and business.

Here are five things you can do to reduce your stress and protect your ability to make sound decisions:

1. **Breathe deeply and reset.** Take slow, deep breaths to calm your nervous system. Breathing helps bring you out of survival mode so you can think clearly.
2. **Step away for clarity.** Go for a short walk or change your environment. Giving yourself space creates the reset your brain needs.
3. **Write it out.** Journaling your thoughts helps you

release the clutter in your mind and regain focus.

4. **Set boundaries.** Say "no" when you need to. Protecting your time and energy reduces unnecessary stress.

5. **Prioritize rest.** Sleep and intentional downtime aren't luxuries. They are leadership tools that restore clarity, focus, and resilience.

Storytime: The High-Stakes Decision That Changed My Life (Deciding to Divorce).

Your home life impacts your work life, your business life, and the decisions you make as a woman leader.

In 2015, I moved to The Azores, Portugal. The place was beautiful: ocean views with sky-blue water, amazing food, welcoming people, and experiences I'll never forget. I was sent there for a year, unaccompanied. That meant it was just me, no kids, no husband at the time. At first, I was disappointed. I wanted my family with me. But once I arrived, I realized I needed that space. Space to breathe, to be alone, to focus on me, to be responsible only for myself and my role as a leader.

Looking back, it was the best decision the Air Force ever

made for me. That year gave me the time to reflect, discover who I was outside of being a mom and wife, and see new possibilities for myself. And in that quiet space, I made one of the hardest, most necessary decisions of my life: to file for divorce after thirteen years of marriage and fifteen years together.

I didn't want to make that decision. It felt heavy because of the impact it would have on my kids, (ages five and ten at the time), and on my husband. But deep down, I knew I needed to choose me. I needed to choose my mental well-being.

Now, imagine the weight: I was leading in another country during a Reduction in Force (RIF). Our organization's manpower was cut drastically, but the workload didn't shrink. I was responsible for a team of junior leaders, 61 civilian employees, and million-dollar resources that had to be transferred or shut down. On top of that, my section managed a budget of $40,000 to build resilience for hundreds of military personnel involved in the RIF. My leadership expected results and I delivered. But the added stress from my personal life? That's what affected how I showed up.

Delaying making the decision to leave my marriage was what truly spiked my stress level. It wasn't just the workload. It was the unhealthy emotional weight that came with it. And I had to face the truth: if I didn't choose me, I would lose me.

Making that decision was painful, but it was also freeing. It allowed me to find myself again, not just as a military leader, not just as a mom or wife, but as Shevvy. The woman who loves life, loves her children, has a vision, and refuses to break under pressure.

And listen, sis, I won't lie to you. It wasn't easy. Even my behavioral counselor, (the one I was referred to because of the stress and the physical tremors I experienced while lying down), looked at me in disbelief. After hearing everything I had endured and how I could still keep it all together, he said, *"Master Sergeant, wow. You could be a great investigator."* He couldn't believe I wasn't falling apart.

But here's the truth: I stayed grounded because I had built my mental resilience. I had no choice. I still had to show up for my kids, even while living in another country. I still had to show up for my team. And I still had to show up for me. That resilience is what kept me together when many women would have been broken.

Sis, I don't want you to break because of your current

circumstances. I want you to breathe through the challenges. Breathe through the tough times. And come out not only standing, but smiling, because you built the resilience to withstand what was designed to break you.

Your growth mindset, your resilience, and your courage to decide, those are the keys that will carry you forward. Whether you're a business owner, professional, parent, partner, wife, or any combination of these roles, you have to decide what actions will keep you whole, healthy, and aligned. Because the life, career, and business you want? They're all on the other side of your decision.

Lessons Learned: Choosing yourself first is a form of self-love. And that act of courage gives you the strength to lead and thrive in every season of life, career, and business.

- Choosing yourself first is an act of self-love, not selfishness.
- Courageous decisions create space for healing and clarity.
- Prioritizing your well-being strengthens your ability to lead with resilience.
- Thriving in life, career, and business begins with the

choice to honor your own needs.

Chapter 4 Decision Tree Activity

Reflection Prompt

What decisions do you need to make today that will shift your life, career, and business for the good and make you a stronger, better woman and leader?

Take this opportunity to complete the following exercise and identify one challenge in each category (Life, Career, Business) that is keeping you from deciding and moving forward. Then, write down the bold step you need to take to start creating the life, career, and business you want.

Instructions:

1. **Identify the Challenge:** Clearly define the challenge you're facing in each area (Life, Career, Business).

2. **State the Objection:** What's holding you back? What are the internal or external objections?

3. **Brainstorm Solutions:** List all possible solutions, even the seemingly unrealistic ones.

4. **Make a Decision:** Based on your reflections, make a decision and outline the next steps.

5. **Next Step:** Decide on your next course of action

Challenge Area: Business	Challenge Area: Life	Challenge Area: Career
What is the challenge?	What is the challenge?	What is the challenge?
What is the objection of this challenge?	What is the objection of this challenge?	What is the objection of this challenge?
What is the one decision you need to make today?	What is the one decision you need to make today?	What is the one decision you need to make today?
What emotions are you experiencing from not making this decision?	What emotions are you experiencing from not making this decision?	What emotions are you experiencing from not making this decision?
What is your desired outcome from making this decision?	What is your desired outcome from making this decision?	What is your desired outcome from making this decision?
What is your next course of action?	What is your next course of action?	What is your next course of action?

Download the decision tree activity by visit www.womanbreathe.com/resources

Strategies for making impactful decisions

Choose yourself first

Prioritize your well-being over people-pleasing. When you put yourself first, you create the space and strength to lead others well. Remember, self-love is not selfish; it's foundational.

Seek wise counsel

Get feedback from others who think and operate at a higher

level. Wise counsel helps you see blind spots, weigh options, and make decisions with greater clarity.

Choosing to remove yourself from people and environments that no longer serve you takes courage and strength. Those very choices shape you into the kind of leader who thrives in any season.

Trust your evidence

Make the best decision with the evidence you have. Stop waiting for every detail to be perfect, or for absolute certainty, because that moment will never come. Trust what you know right now and take the step forward.

"Stress doesn't have to control you. When you choose to manage it with intention, you reclaim your power and gain the strength to show up fully; not just for others, but for yourself."

Chapter 5: Stress Management for Leading with Resilience

Understanding the Body's Stress Response and Its Impact on Leadership

Your body and mind go through so much when you're under extreme stress. You're probably aware of what you're experiencing but, like I once did, you may not be fully acknowledging it. When your body is under an enormous amount of stress there are neurological shifts, physical shifts, and emotional shifts happening inside of you.

Let's break them down:

- **Neurological shifts** may show up as mental fog, consistent headaches, unexplained body pain, dizziness, or pressure in your head.

- **Physical shifts** might look like weight gain or weight loss, fatigue, dark circles under your eyes, irritability, poor appetite, or frequent angry outbursts.

- **Emotional shifts** can appear as anxiety, depression, overwhelm, fear, anger, isolation, or uncontrollable crying.

If you're experiencing one or more of these right now, I want you to pause. Take 60 seconds and write down what you are feeling. What words best describe your emotions in this moment?

This simple exercise is powerful. It helps you acknowledge the emotions you're carrying. And when you acknowledge them, you create space to own them and then decide how to act. That's the first step toward building your **Stress Management Blueprint™**.

Remember, stress can sometimes be useful. Certain stressors actually strengthen your resilience. But too much stress, left unchecked, will lead you down an unhealthy path, impacting your mental well-being and slowing down your development as a resilient woman leader in life, career, and business.

Stress Management Blueprint™
This blueprint is your tool to reduce stress and help you show up and lead well in all areas of your life:

- Five minutes of quiet time (no interruptions)

- Five minutes of dancing by yourself or with someone you love
- Read your favorite book again, or discover a new one
- Five minutes of positive self-talk
- Take yourself out for lunch
- Five minutes of gratitude (say it out loud, silently, or write it down)
- Five minutes of listening to your favorite song(s)
- Schedule a 60- to 90-minute massage
- Take a mini solo trip (3 hours a day, or a few days)
- Hop on a bike, roller skates, or tap into your inner child for 30 minutes
- Go to the park and play on at least three items (swing, slide, etc.)
- Free FLOW: be creative and do something just for you!

As you navigate life, career, and business, the goal is not to overextend yourself to the point of collapse, multiple ER visits, burnout or worse, serious health conditions like depression, heart attack, or stroke. That's not the path we're choosing. This is your awakening.

Be honest with yourself. What do you need to acknowledge today so you can finally act? Because when you act, you change how you lead, not just today, but tomorrow, and into your future.

It's not about saying, *"I need to make a Stress Management Blueprint."* It's about declaring, *"I have a Stress Management Blueprint, and I'm using it."*

Becoming a resilient woman leader means you know when to pause, when to breathe, and when to take care of yourself, especially when life gets tough, when your career feels overwhelming, and when your business demands more than you think you have to give.

You already have the mental resilience inside you. This is about protecting it, nurturing it, and refusing to let stress dictate the quality of your life. It's time to take control of your life, career, and business, and it starts with you.

Women and stress statistics that validate why you must manage or reduce your stress.

Woman, Breathe

Statistic	What It Shows	Source
Women who say stress affects their health "a lot" have a 43% higher risk of premature death.	Perceived stress isn't just "in your head"—it has measurable mortality impact.	Keller, A. et al., *Does the Perception that Stress Affects Health Matter?* PMC
43% of female executives report burnout, vs. 31% of male executives.	Women in leadership report more chronic stress and exhaustion.	McKinsey, *Women in the Workplace 2024* via International Women's Day, ie.edu
Women report more symptoms of stress (headaches, upset stomach, mental health issues).	Stress manifests more physically and mentally in women than men.	U.S. Office on Women's Health
Chronic stress in women links to heart	Validates the neurological and	American Heart Association,

Statistic	What It Shows	Source
disease, high blood pressure, and higher heart rate.	physical burden of stress.	*Women and Stress*, heart.org

Creating a Personalized Stress Management Plan

Deciding to create a personalized Stress Management Plan needs to be a top priority as you navigate life, career, and business. At the end of the day, you can't keep crying behind closed doors, breaking down in your car because you're at your wits' end. You can't keep running on empty, showing up for everyone else while neglecting yourself.

If you're not managing your stress and don't have resources you can tap into when you're overwhelmed and burned out, you'll reach a point where you simply don't have the capacity to give anymore to anyone or anything. That's why you need your own Stress Management Plan, your own toolbox. It's a gift to yourself, a box you can reach into when you need a reset, when you need to breathe.

Taking time to pause and catch your breath helps you step back and consciously re-center yourself. It gives you the space to ask, *"What do I need right now to take care of me?"*

Too often, we pour everything we have into others, and no one is pouring back into us.

I was there. Honestly, sometimes I'm still there. I've had to remind myself to tap into my Stress Management Toolbox. For me, movement is one of my go-to gifts. I make time for it at least five times a week. Movement helps me recenter my body, reset my mind, reignite my energy, and reduce mental fatigue. It's what keeps me strong, resilient, and grounded.

Now it's your turn. I want you to identify what belongs in *your* Stress Management Toolbox.

Chapter 5 Reflective Activity 1
What are five things you can add to your Stress Management Toolbox that help you reset, breathe, and rebuild your resilience?

Chapter 5 Reflective Activity 2
Reflection Activity: Build Your Stress Management Toolbox
Instructions:
Take a moment to think about your current stress load. Then, use the prompts below to create your personalized toolbox.

Area	What Helps Me Reset?	Why This Matters to Me	How Often Can I Commit to This?
Tool 1			
Tool 2			
Tool 3			
Tool 4			
Tool 5			

Tip: Think small and sustainable. Your toolbox doesn't have to be complicated; it just needs to include things that bring you calm, clarity, and energy when life feels heavy.

Storytime: Showing Up Like Everything is Normal, Even Though You're Screaming Inside. (I had already been hospitalized before.)

I was an instructor at Fort Lee Army base from 2010 to 2013. During that time, I was still dealing with anxiety after being admitted to the hospital for vertigo a few weeks before arriving at Fort Lee from Lackland Air Force Base in San Antonio, Texas.

As an instructor, my mornings were routine: drop my daughter off at the bus stop in the neighborhood (she was in kindergarten), then drop my son off at daycare on base. My son was about seven or eight months old then. After I dropped him off, I drove to work, parked in the lot, and that's when it would start: my heart would begin racing.

Walking into the building felt like a battle. My heart rate spiked, my alertness shot up, and my body and mind began shifting, emotionally, neurologically, physically. As I rode the elevator up, I remember telling myself not to freak out in front of my co-workers. A few people were holding the elevator door for me, and suddenly I felt claustrophobic. I couldn't breathe. I just wanted to get out.

When the elevator doors opened, I felt a sliver of relief. I was fighting my own inner turmoil, trying to suppress the emotions and sensations instead of owning them and managing my stress. I was physically there, but mentally checked out. Still, I showed up for my role. I taught. I trained twenty-six young military students eight hours a day, five days a week, often for six-week rotations. Sometimes I graduated from one class one day and welcomed another the next. I showed up for them like nothing was wrong.

But after teaching, after presenting, my anxiety would rush back in. I experienced neurological symptoms: dizziness, the walls feeling like they were shifting. It was terrifying. And yet I kept going. Too often, this is what we do as women: we carry it, we hide it, and we keep showing up.

A Simple Exercise to See Where You Are

Let's pause for a moment and get real with yourself.

- Are you feeling the symptoms?
- Do you feel light-headed consistently?
- Is your heart pounding and racing randomly?
- Do you find it hard to lie down and actually fall asleep, or stay asleep, because you're jumping awake in panic?
- Do you ever feel like you're about to have a heart attack?
- At what point will you say *enough is enough*?

As ambitious and driven women, we want so much for ourselves. We're visionaries. We carry the weight for others. And we keep showing up, even when we're struggling internally with our own *ish*. But here's the truth: it's time to shift the narrative. It's time to rewrite the outcome of how you're showing up in your life, your career, and your business.

Storytime: My Breaking Point - Learning to Manage Stress the Hard Way

I want to share another time when I was under an enormous amount of stress while stationed in Portugal. As you already know, I was leading through a base reduction in force (RIF), responsible for people, resources, and constant demands. On top of that, the pressure of my personal life added even more weight. I kept pushing through, just like you might be doing right now- strong, ambitious, and determined to show up no matter what.

But my body had other plans. After a long day of holding it all together, I lay down one evening and suddenly the room started spinning. The same terrifying vertigo symptoms I had experienced before came rushing back. My heart was racing, the walls felt like they were shifting, and I felt completely out of control. I had to call a friend to stay with me, but when things got worse, she rushed me to the ER in Portugal. My blood pressure was higher than normal, and my body was sending me a clear message: *enough is enough.* Maybe your body is doing the same thing to you right now.

That was my breaking point. I realized I couldn't keep living in a cycle of stress without consequences. If I had continued, I might have ended up with a stroke or worse. That moment forced me to self-evaluate. I had to ask myself the hard questions: *What can I control? How am I responding? Who am I allowing into my space?*

I'm sharing this with you because unmanaged stress doesn't just stay in your head. It attacks your body, your health, and your future. Don't wait until you're in the ER to make a change. Listen to your body. Respect the signals.

Right now, I want you to complete this reflective activity. It's simple, but it will give you clarity on how to start showing up for *you*, so that when you show up for others you're no longer pouring from an empty cup.

Chapter 5 Reflective Activity 3:
- Who are you still showing up for during your crises?
- How do you plan to show up today and tomorrow that's different from how you're currently showing up for others?
- Take five minutes and write down how you plan to show up for yourself today and tomorrow, so you can navigate your life, your career, and your business without losing yourself.

Lessons Learned: Managing stress is not optional; it prevents fear, burnout, and poor performance. When you manage stress well, you lead with resilience in every season of life, career, and business.

Managing stress is not optional. Stress left unchecked leads to fear, burnout, and poor performance, and it will impact how you show up as a woman leader.

Stress management protects your resilience. By caring for your mind and body, you create the capacity to make clear decisions, lead effectively, and sustain your energy.

Resilient leadership starts with you. When you intentionally manage stress, you not only prevent breakdown, you also position yourself to thrive in every season of life, career, and business.

Strategies for getting out of the burnout zone:

Identify your stress signals
Notice how your body warns you when you're stepping into a high-stress zone. It might show up as tension in your shoulders, a racing heart, or constant irritability. Paying attention to these early signals gives you the chance to step back and address stress before it overwhelms you.

Apply the Stress Management Blueprint™
Don't just notice stress, take action. Use the strategies from your Stress Management Blueprint™ to restore balance. Whether it's five minutes of quiet time, movement, or

gratitude, these small but intentional actions help you reset your energy and keep moving forward with clarity.

Build a recovery practice

Make recovery a daily habit, not an afterthought. Breathwork, journaling, short breaks, or even simple affirmations can become your go-to tools for resilience. Consistently practicing recovery allows you to show up stronger, calmer, and more focused in every area of life, career, and business.

Stress doesn't have to control you. When you choose to manage it with intention, you reclaim your power and gain the strength to show up fully, not just for others, but for yourself. That's the foundation of resilience and the key to leading well in every season of life, career, and business.

Chapter 5 Reflective Activity 4:

What signals are your body giving you right now? Write them down and ask yourself what needs to shift before your body decides for you.

Action Assignment: Want to take your stress management further? Send me a direct message on LinkedIn at Shevon 'Shevvy" Maxwell with the word **"Beyond"** to learn about the **Go Beyond Management Leadership Training Program**, a certified program by the Optimind Institute. This training equips managers and executive leaders with practical tools to manage stress, strengthen resilience, and lead with real-world readiness.

"Your team is the backbone of your organization and your business."

Part 3: Stewardship: Leadership & Influence- Practical Leadership Strategies for Building a Resilient Culture

Chapter 6: Building & Leading Resilient Teams

How to Foster Resilience in Your Team

Your team is the backbone of your organization and your business. If your team isn't able to function because of the stress and chaos of life and work, then they can't show up as their best selves or deliver on the roles they were hired to execute.

As the leader, it's up to you to foster, create, and develop a resilient team and that starts with understanding your people. When you truly understand your team, you get to build genuine connections and trust. You're able to empathize and recognize their challenges without judgment. You're able to communicate with clarity while still holding strong boundaries. And you're able to lead with compassion when your team members are walking through difficult life or work situations.

When you take this approach, you and your team get to co-create a workplace culture that not only increases performance but also supports a better quality of life.

Leading With Confidence
Leading comes naturally for some and feels more challenging for others. For me, I love leading. I love empowering others to step fully into their role and build the systems, structures, and solutions that bring their big vision to life.

That doesn't mean I haven't faced challenges. I've had plenty, during my military career and in my business. But each of those experiences shaped me into a stronger leader across every area of my life. And I want the same for you.

When you face leadership challenges, I want you to see them as opportunities for growth. That's how you build resilience, not just in yourself, but in your team.

Here are some practical ways to help foster resilience in your team:

- Create transparency in communication- Encourage open dialogue so your team feels safe sharing their challenges with you.
- Build psychological safety- Create an environment

where mistakes can be admitted, vulnerabilities can be shared, and personal challenges like family issues, grief, or divorce aren't ignored. If those things aren't acknowledged, your team can't mentally show up to do their work well.

- Empower decision-making- Give your team the chance to make strategic decisions under pressure. This builds confidence and leadership capacity.

- Encourage risk-taking- Let them test ideas, learn what worked, and own what didn't.

- Challenge your team- Stretch them beyond their comfort zones so they grow stronger at handling tough situations and decisions under pressure.

- Create a thriving culture- Foster an environment where your team feels they can overcome challenges, take risks, be innovative, and challenge the norms. Put resources in place that allow them to think critically and bring real solutions.

- Share leadership opportunities- Give team members the chance to lead without micromanaging, based on trust.

- Incentivize their commitment- Recognize their performance, dedication, and initiative without them having to ask. When your team knows you see them, they'll go above and beyond for your vision.

- Protect their reset time- Notice when your team is giving you extra, coming early, staying late, and make sure they have time to rest and reset, not just on weekends.

- Invite collaboration and creativity- Create opportunities for your team to reset together outside of the work environment. This helps them recharge mentally, emotionally, and physically so they can return ready to give their best.

At the end of the day, you're the leader. It's your responsibility to create the space, provide the resources, and offer the opportunities that allow your team to be resilient and overcome challenges.

I'm not saying leadership is easy, but I am saying that when you lead with intention, **you can make leadership something you love, no matter the environment or the people you're leading.**

Storytime: Leading Through Change and Uncertainty

It was September 2016, and I was preparing to close out my military tour in Portugal. It was Labor Day weekend and, for three days, I had nothing but time to be alone with my thoughts. I paced back and forth in my bedroom, wrestling with a decision that I knew would change everything: how was I going to tell my husband that I wanted a divorce?

It wasn't easy. I knew it would devastate our kids. But I thought about everything I had endured, the manipulation, the disrespect, the stress. And I finally gathered the courage to pick up the phone, open WhatsApp, and softly say the words: *"I want a divorce."*

Of course, he replied that he didn't want one. But for me, my mind was made up. I had replayed the last 15 years of our relationship over and over, and I knew it was time. I was done. I wanted more for myself, and the marriage wasn't part of that future anymore.

Afterward, I felt a sigh of relief. But that didn't erase the difficulty of what was ahead, because kids were involved. And young kids.

As I transitioned back to the States to pick up my kids and

prepare to move them to Europe, I knew it was going to be a mental and emotional battle. My ex-husband had already planted seeds in their minds. He told my daughter, "Mommy wanted a divorce," so naturally, their anger and hurt were directed at me. The looks they gave me, especially my daughter, pierced my heart. It was part of his manipulation, and it made an already painful process even harder.

By the time we got to the airport to fly to Europe, emotions were everywhere. The kids were about to leave the country without their dad, and now they had to accept that mom and dad were no longer together. I felt their pain. I felt their confusion. I was hurting too. But I had to stay strong, for them, and for me.

Through the entire divorce process, from the first conversation to the final decision by the judge, I stayed resilient by leaning on my mindset. Yes, there were moments when I broke down. I cried in the shower. I had nights where my stress was so high that lying down felt like the bed was rocking like a boat in the middle of the ocean. My blood pressure, my nerves, my body all carried the weight of it.

But I didn't let that stop me from showing up. I showed up for my kids, making sure they felt loved and safe. I showed up for my work, continuing to lead my team. I showed up for my community, staying connected instead of isolating myself. And most importantly, I showed up for myself.

That season taught me one of the hardest lessons of my life: people will only do what you allow them to do. Some will try to break you mentally, emotionally, and spiritually until you can't find yourself anymore. But when you tap into your resilience, when you learn to strengthen your self-talk and shift your perspective, no one can break you.

Lessons Learned

When you trust yourself as a leader, you gain the confidence and resilience to guide your team through change and uncertainty. Trust allows you to create a culture of openness and psychological safety where your people can thrive.

Resilient leadership also means:

- Building genuine connections with your team so they know they can come to you without judgment.

- Creating transparency in communication so challenges can be addressed before they spiral.

- Empowering your team to take risks, learn, and grow into leaders

Strategy for building resilient teams

Lead your team to respond well by showing composure and clarity yourself. When they see you steady under pressure, it gives them permission to stay grounded and resilient too. Your presence sets the tone; if you panic, they will panic; if you remain calm, they will mirror your calm. Resilience is caught, not just taught, and it starts with the example you set daily.

Lead with confidence

Believe in yourself so your team can believe in you. Confidence doesn't mean having all the answers; it means trusting your ability to navigate challenges and guide your team through them. When you show up with certainty and courage, you create a sense of stability that your team needs in uncertain times. Your confidence reminds them that setbacks are temporary, and solutions are always within reach.

Develop your people

Invest in building skills and culture that enable your team to perform at a high level under pressure. When you prioritize their growth, you strengthen their resilience and elevate the entire team. Development happens in training sessions, but also in the feedback you give, the opportunities you create, and the trust you extend. A resilient team is one that feels equipped, valued, and empowered to rise to every challenge.

Client Testimony: Jerry was dealing with communication breakdown among different levels of leadership and different styles of leading.

Jerry St. Pierre · 1st
Active Duty Chaplain, US Air Force/ President, The St. Pierre Alliance / Owner, Cozy Properties of North Georgia, LLC
April 20, 2022, Jerry was Shevvy Mac's client

Shevvy Mac was instrumental in helping my office team understand our team dynamics and develop tools to improve overall interpersonal relationships. She dynamically led us through a four hour session integrating coaching and neuroscience skill to help us analyze our leadership and team and to develop a way forward that yielded positive results.

Because of her outstanding performance, I invited her to coach me as I launched The St. Pierre Alliance.

During this time, Shevvy Mac served as a sounding board for my ideas, and she challenged my limiting beliefs contributing to a successful launch!

She has been an asset to our organization, and I recommend her services.

The resilience of your team is a reflection of your leadership. When you choose to model strength, lead with confidence, and pour into your people, you're not just building a team; you're building leaders who can thrive in any environment.

Chapter 6 Reflective Activity: Team Resilience Reflection

- Write down three specific challenges your team is

facing right now.

- For each challenge, list one action you can take as the leader to support your team through it.
- Share this with your team (or keep it as your own guide) and revisit it in 30 days to measure progress.

Action Assignment: Download your guide: *The Five Biggest Mistakes High-Performing Small Business Owners Make That Keep Them from Stepping into Their CEO Role.* Use it to identify what may be holding your leadership back and how to strengthen your team's resilience. Scan the QR Code titled The 5 biggest mistakes business owners are making to download your guide.

"Your ability to communicate creates change, drives action, and sets the tone for how others experience your leadership."

Chapter 7: Leading Through Communication and Managing Conflict

The Role of Communication in Resilient Leadership

As a business owner or professional leader, the way you communicate with yourself, your team, and your customers shapes the health of your business' or organization's culture, outcomes, and impact. When communication breaks down, stress multiplies for you, for your team, and for everyone connected to you.

If you're stepping into being a resilient and transformational leader, your communication becomes one of your core competencies. Your ability to communicate creates change, drives action, and sets the tone for how others experience your leadership. The ability to speak with clarity, confidence, and compassion at every level not only drives your success but also drives your team's success.

Open and healthy communication leads to stronger workplace cultures, higher productivity, fewer errors, deeper connections, and greater collaboration among team members.

Understanding Communication Styles
Effective communication starts with recognizing the different styles: yours and your team's. Ask yourself:

- Are you a direct leader who can correct individuals and say exactly what needs to be said without being mean or nasty?

- Are you the type who can stay calm and respond effectively under different levels of stress?

- Or are you the leader who feels the need to know everything and micromanage?

Your answers matter because the way you lead and the way you communicate directly impact how your team responds to you. When you try to be "in all the things," you overload yourself mentally and emotionally. You burn more energy making decisions and processing details. And when your mind is stretched thin, you unintentionally create an environment where your team struggles to perform effectively. You can't be the leader who has to carry every single decision on your own.

Communicating Through Conflict

No matter your environment, conflict will arise. And as a leader, you can't run from it; you have to welcome it, control it, and create space for healthy resolution. Conflict resolution is a critical leadership skill because it showcases resilience and competence.

When leaders avoid conflict, they weaken trust, respect, and accountability within the team. But when you face conflict directly, with an open mind, you create opportunities for dialogue, problem-solving, and growth. You also model for your team how to handle challenges in a healthy, professional way.

Effective communication and conflict resolution drive innovation, success, resilience, and a healthier workplace culture. As a leader, it's your responsibility to ensure that every voice on your team is heard and validated. That doesn't mean every opinion will be right, but it does mean that people feel safe enough to share their thoughts. And remember, some voices are naturally louder, so it's important to make room for the quieter ones.

Recognizing the Voice Types on Your Team
Every team is made up of different "voice types." Recognizing them helps you communicate more effectively:

- **The Visionary**: Sees the big picture, speaks up with bold ideas, and isn't afraid to challenge the status quo.

- **The Builder:** Creates connections, brings people together, and sparks collaboration inside and outside the team.

- **The Caregiver:** Focuses on emotional health, impact, and team well-being, often preferring to stay out of the spotlight.

- **The Protector:** Grounded in facts, structure, and logic. Values efficiency, clarity, and reducing waste.

- **The Developer:** Generates creative solutions and isn't shy about voicing what's working and what's not.

Ask yourself:

- What is your voice type?
- How does it differ from your team members'?

- As a leader, how are you communicating with yourself and your team to create a healthy, resilient workplace?

- What are three things you can implement today to start communicating more effectively?

Storytime: Navigating Conflict While Remaining Calm

Over my twenty-two-plus years in the United States Air Force, I've had all kinds of leaders. Some were great, some were ineffective. And what I've learned is this: being in a position of leadership will test your character every single day. Some days, you may want to put hands on somebody, but you know you can't. I know I did. Mentally, I did, but never physically.

There was one leader in particular who stood out when it came to being an ineffective communicator and a conflict starter. Let's call him Sergeant Sam. From day one at Lajes Air Base in the Azores, Portugal, it was clear that his communication style was toxic. He thought he was "Mr. Know-It-All," even though he wasn't in my line of work. We were in the same organization, but in different career fields.

Within my first week of arriving, I was already hearing from others about the issues Sergeant Sam caused. And it didn't take long before I experienced it myself. Even though we were technically on the same leadership level, he tried to talk down to me like I was his subordinate. But I wasn't having that. I made it clear, with emotional intelligence, that he was not going to talk to me disrespectfully.

We butted heads often, and eventually a mediator was brought in. But the truth was, it was a lost cause. Sergeant Sam wasn't interested in resolving anything. He only wanted things his way. At that point, I made a decision for myself: I would regulate my emotions, keep communication with him strictly job-related, and remove myself from any unnecessary interaction.

Some leaders and team members will create chaos in your life, career, and business. They will test your patience, your well-being, and your resilience. But the way you respond, that's what matters. When you choose to regulate yourself, you protect your peace and preserve your credibility.

When you use your voice to communicate with clarity and self-control, you step fully into being the resilient woman leader you're called to be. You show that you can communicate under pressure, with anyone, at any level. And you set the tone for your team and your culture. Because at the end of the day, your communication has the power to either destroy or build resilience, both in you and in those you lead.

Lessons Learned
Your communication as a leader has the power to either build or break resilience, trust, and growth. The words you choose, the tone you use, and the way you carry yourself will set the atmosphere for your team, your business, and even your family. If you communicate with clarity, respect, and empathy, you create a culture where people feel safe to share ideas, admit mistakes, and push through challenges together.

But when communication is careless, when tone is sharp, dismissive, or inconsistent, you weaken trust. You add unnecessary stress. You create confusion instead of clarity. Over time, this doesn't just damage relationships; it erodes performance, innovation, and the resilience of your entire team.

The lesson is this: as a resilient woman leader, you have to be intentional with your communication at all times. That doesn't mean you'll always get it perfect, but it does mean you pause, check yourself, and choose words that lead to growth, not destruction. Every conversation is an opportunity to strengthen your leadership and to show your team how to rise above conflict with grace and confidence

Strategies for Effective Communication
Use all three channels

Communication isn't just about the words you speak. It's also about your visuals, your tone, and your body language. Each one sends a message. Lead with intention in all three areas, so what you say matches how you say it and how you show up.

Check your approach

Take time to reflect on how you handle conflict in life, career, and business. Do you shut down? Do you explode? Or do you respond with calm authority? Your approach matters because it sets the tone for your team and determines whether conflict leads to growth or division.

Know your people

Get to know your team on a personal level. Learn what motivates them, what challenges them, and how they best receive information. When you understand the people you lead, you build trust, and trust creates the foundation for resilience and high performance.

Client Testimony: (Iris, understand her voice type so she can operate in her zone to grow her business.) Iris was at a point in her business where she wanted to be more visible on social media and build out her signature coaching program.

Before hiring me, Iris had no visibility and was not comfortable posting or showing her face on social media.

After working together for three months, Iris increased her visibility by 100%, grew her engagement, and launched her LinkedIn Audio Series where she consistently increased her attendees.

Due to her newfound visibility, a university reached out and offered her an opportunity that leveraged her coaching and counseling background.

Every conversation, and every conflict, is a chance to lead with clarity, calm, and resilience. When you choose to communicate with intention, you don't just resolve problems, you strengthen trust, build culture, and create growth. Remember, your words carry power. Use them to lead yourself, your team, and your business forward.

Chapter 7 Reflective Activity:

Here's a set of activities that tie directly to communication and conflict resolution:

Activity 1: Communication Audit

- Reflect on your last 5 important conversations (team, family, or friends).
- For each, ask yourself: Did I lead with clarity? Did my body language align with my words? Did I listen fully before responding?
- Write down one thing you could have improved in each conversation.

Activity 2: Conflict Role-Play (Self-Reflection)

- Write out a recent or recurring conflict you've had.
- Now, write two scripts: how you initially responded, and how you *wish* you had responded with resilience and calm.
- Compare the two and identify the difference in tone, words, and outcome.

Action Assignment: Turn to the **Voice Types above**. Take this time to identify your own voice type and compare it with those of your team. Notice how your style shapes the way you lead, influence, and resolve conflict.

> ***"Resilience, flexibility, and the ability to thrive without losing yourself are the keys to building a sustainable business."***

Chapter 8: Operating With Purpose

Your Purpose

I am a visionary, builder, connector, and executor. When I see something I want, I go after it and implement it. I'm multi-passionate, which means I love doing many things that inspire me and allow me to make an impact in the lives and communities of others.

My very first business was as a Notary in Minot, North Dakota. It only lasted several months because after paying the fees and getting a few jobs, I was selected to move to Portugal, Azores, for my year-long tour.

My second business, *MAC Wellness*, came out of my personal battle with anxiety. When I decided to make myself a priority, I focused on getting my health together. That meant educating myself on nutrition, eating cleaner, practicing positive self-talk, incorporating movement, and journaling. Those four strategies became my foundation for managing my anxiety instead of letting it manage me.

Out of this drive, I began sharing my exercise videos, smoothies, and recipes on YouTube. Click the QR Code below title Wellness video to see where it all started. I had always wanted a YouTube channel where I could share the things that helped me release anxiety. I also posted on Instagram and Facebook. There wasn't much traction, no money coming in, not many views, but I kept showing up. That's what leaders do: we keep showing up through life, career, and business, even when the results aren't immediate.

As time went on, I wanted to bring what I was doing forward to others. At first, I didn't even think of it as a business. It felt more like blogging. But I went ahead and got an EIN for *MAC Wellness*, purchased my first domain (*ShevvyMac.com*), built my own website, and officially launched it. I still remember publishing my very first blog at 1 a.m. while deployed to Turkey. That blog became my starting point. I wrote about life and wellness, shared tips, exercises, and recipes.

When I reflect back on my childhood in Guyana and New Jersey, I realize entrepreneurship has always been part of me. I grew up watching my mom step into entrepreneurship long before I even understood the word. In Guyana, when I was about six or seven, she sold food and drinks, and even made baskets from scratch to sell. My siblings and I helped her, whether it was weaving baskets or running small sales stands. I remember my sister Shawnette and I setting up by the draw bridge near my home when it was closed to cars, selling chips, candies, water, and small items. Most days we sold out.

That memory stayed with me. When I look back now, I see clearly: entrepreneurship has always been in part of my DNA. But let's be real: being an entrepreneur is not easy, especially when you're balancing career, family, and business. Yet, every part of my journey, whether as a notary, a wellness blogger, or building something bigger, was leading me back to my purpose.

Release the Doubts
As I built my business, there were times when I questioned

myself. *When is my turn coming? When will I start signing consistent clients and bringing in consistent money?* I would say to myself, *"I have all this talent from my military experience. I am about people first. I can help so many people. Why aren't they coming to me for my services?"*

I would see other women thriving in their space who didn't have the skillset or experience I had, but I still kept going on my journey of entrepreneurship. And let me tell you, it's hard when you know your skill level, your execution, and your dedication are on another level, but maybe others are better at sales.

In those early days, I became frustrated. I shed tears. I questioned why it wasn't working for me. What I realized as I kept building was this: I had the talent and the skillset, but what I didn't have was *clear positioning and messaging* on who I served and the results I provided. On top of that, I bounced from coach to coach because their approach didn't resonate with them me at the beginning of my entrepreneurial journey.

But here's what I've learned over the years: you have to be clear, you have to be intentional, and you have to know exactly who you serve and how you serve them.

When I started my business, I was still on active duty in the Air Force. And as I continued to build, I had my third child, earned my real estate license, and even enrolled in a doctoral program while my youngest was under two years old. At that point, I had to give myself grace and put that program on pause.

As I continue on this journey to build a multi-million dollar company, my resilience has to remain at the forefront. It's what has carried me through the ups and downs of being a full-time entrepreneur.

Like you, I've poured in my time, energy, and money, even when things didn't go as planned. But I kept my vision front and center, and I stayed rooted in a growth mindset. And that's what I want you to remember: you will get frustrated, you will shed tears, you will doubt yourself, and you will face fears and uncertainties. But through it all, resilience, flexibility, and the ability to thrive without losing yourself *are* the keys to building a sustainable business.

Storytime: Using Your Life and Career Experiences to Launch Your Business and Operate in Your Purpose Through the Challenges of Life and Career

Building Resilience to Keep Going in Your Business
Entrepreneurship is not for the faint of heart.

Entrepreneurship is for you if you're willing to take risks. It's for you if you're willing to invest financially- small, medium, or big investments- invest your time, and keep going even when things aren't moving in the direction you expected.

Since launching my business, I've shifted from *MAC Wellness* to *MAC Leadership Academy*, where I now offer leadership consulting, leadership development, people development, and training for businesses and organizations. I've served different individuals and organizations throughout this journey, and I'm still building. Resilience is what has carried me through the ups and downs of business ownership.

I have spent thousands of dollars on training, coaching, consulting, workshops, and conferences to grow my business, because my vision isn't short-term, it's long-term. I want you to think the same way. My return on investment (ROI) wasn't immediate. It took years before I started seeing real traction. If I hadn't been resilient in the way I moved and thought, I wouldn't be here writing this book for you. I wouldn't even have a business.

If I weren't resilient, I would have given up a long time ago. I've been building and investing in my business since I hired my first coach in March 2020. This journey hasn't been easy, and I know it hasn't been easy for you either. I've learned a lot of lessons, good and bad. From making a five-figure investment with no financial ROI in 2020… to signing my biggest five-figure client in 2024.

And that only happened because I believed in the vision. I believed in the impact that *MAC Leadership Academy* would have on women like you, women navigating life, career, and business, while also supporting organizational leaders. That's how you need to view your business too: with big vision, big outcomes, and big sustainability.

Lessons Learned

Operating in your purpose takes clarity, intention, and grace. When you have clarity, you unlock the strength to thrive in every season of life, career, and business.

Operating in your purpose takes clarity. You can't build on confusion. The more intentional you are about your vision, the stronger your path becomes.

Give yourself grace. Building a business isn't overnight; it's a process of resilience, trial, error, and growth.

Your why is your anchor. When challenges hit, it's the reason you started that will keep you going.

Your strengths are your superpower. Lean on them, lead from them, and use them to create impact.

Release limits. Fear, comparison, and doubt will try to hold you back, but they can't survive when you choose to keep showing up in your purpose.

Strategies for operating in your zone of genius

1. **Return to your why**
   Reconnect with the reason behind your journey. When things feel heavy or unclear, remind yourself of why you started. Your why gives you direction when the path feels uncertain.

2. **Use your strengths**
   Your strength is your superpower, so lead from it. Lean into the unique skills, experiences, and gifts that make you different. When you operate in your strengths, you build confidence and create impact more naturally.

3. **Release limits**

   Let go of beliefs that keep you from walking fully in your purpose. Doubt, fear, and comparison will try to shrink you, but you get to decide differently. The moment you release those limits, you create space for clarity, growth, and alignment.

Client Testimony: Sara came to me because she was uncertain and needed clarity on her career as a military spouse and during our one-hour intensive, she was able to gain clarity on how she could use her degrees in food science to help businesses grow.

Purpose isn't found in the perfect moment; it's built in the messy ones. When you operate with clarity, intention, and grace, you stop chasing and start leading. Your purpose isn't waiting on you to be perfect; it's waiting on you to show up.

Chapter 8 Reflective Activity:

Here's Your Opportunity to Go Deeper on Your Business or Career "Why"

This exercise is your chance to tap back into your *why*, especially if you're feeling uncertain about continuing in your business. It's here to help you reflect on what truly matters, how you want to spend your time, and the kind of impact you want your business to create.

Take a few minutes to sit with these questions and be honest with yourself:

- What is your why?
- Why did you start your business or career that you have?
- **What strengths do you lean on in difficult times?**
- How do you want to spend your time in your business or career?
- What do you want to spend *more* of your time on?

- **What are three things you would love to accomplish in your business in the next 6 to 12 months?**

- **What are three things you would love to accomplish in your career in the next 6 to 12 months?**

Remember, your "why" is bigger than profit. It's about purpose, alignment, and the impact you're here to make.

Action Assignment: Operating in Your Purpose Activity: Write down your top three strengths, your biggest limiting belief, and your why. Then answer: How can I use my strengths to silence that belief and stay aligned with my why this week?

"Thriving in every season doesn't mean doing it alone. Resilient leadership requires you to seek help early, prioritize your well-being, and build habits that fuel both your body and your mind."

Part 4: Sustainability: Growth & Alignment - Lifestyle Strategies for Sustained Resilience

Chapter 9: Lifestyle Habits for Resilient Leadership

Nourishing Your Brain for Performance

As you navigate life, career, and business, it's easy to lose track of time because you're inundated with the responsibilities of leading others, making decisions, supporting family, meeting deadlines, and juggling everything else. And when you're that busy, you don't always nourish your mind and body the way you should.

I know, because I've been there. In the past, I've skipped meals, not intentionally, but because I was working full-time on active duty, going to school, parenting, and building my business. Time slipped away. When I did remember to eat, I grabbed foods that didn't fuel me. Instead of sustaining my mental energy and clarity, they drained me.

But here's the truth: you have to make time to sustain *you*. If you want to build a healthy, resilient mind, you must fuel your brain with foods that boost performance. The type of foods you eat directly impacts your brain energy, focus, and clarity, which determines your ability to make sound decisions as a leader. When you're not feeding your brain and body properly, the opposite happens. You lose clarity, your decision-making slows down, and your ability to process, analyze, and think logically decreases.

I learned this the hard way during my journey with anxiety. I had to rebuild my mental resilience, and what I consumed played a critical role. The right foods cleared my mental fog and gave me the energy to keep leading, managing teams, running operations, and making countless personal and professional decisions, all while sustaining myself.

Here's what neuroscience tells us: our brain consumes about 20% of our body's total energy. That means 20% of the food you eat goes straight to fueling your brain. (Shonté Jovan Taylor, *Optimind Institute*). What you eat affects your brain function, your mood, and ultimately your leadership performance.

If you eat well, you fuel your clarity and energy. If you don't, you increase stress and your risk of developing health problems like high blood pressure. As women leaders, we often put everyone else first- family, work, and community- because we care. But when we don't prioritize ourselves, burnout creeps in.

Stress from my military and life experiences had triggered anxiety and high blood pressure, but lifestyle changes helped me reset. For me, food became medicine. By eating more holistically, I reduced my anxiety symptoms, cleared my mind, gained natural energy, and even lowered my blood pressure. What you consume affects your mindset, and your mindset determines your ability to be resilient. The wrong foods can drag you into a mental dark space. But the right ones can lift you up, helping you manage thoughts, energy, and clarity so you can lead effectively.

To help you get started, I created a **30-Day Holistic Guide** that I've used myself and with clients to build clarity, lose weight, and enhance mental energy. This guide is your first step toward supporting your mind, body, and leadership so you can thrive as a resilient woman leader.

Your Next Step: The 30-Day Wellness Plan: A Self-Led Journey to Thrive in Every Season™

I created a **30-Day Holistic Guide** that I've used for myself and with clients to build clarity, reduce stress, lose weight, and enhance mental energy. Turn your five-day reset, lead, and thrive challenge -that is provided to individuals who purchase the book bundle- into a full 30-day lifestyle, nourish your mind, body, and balance with intention every day.

Get your digital copy by scanning the QR Code below to shift your well-being.

Sleep and Resilience to Lead Better
Sleep is not a luxury; it's a necessity for your brain and body to reset. While on active duty, there were days when I worked twelve-plus hours, whether at my main duty station or in a deployed environment. We often pushed twelve to fourteen hours straight for multiple days because the mission had to get done. During those times, yes, your body will keep

going because it has to, but the moment you stop, the crash comes. Without proper rest, you lose the mental clarity needed to make sound decisions. You become irritable, foggy, and reactive instead of calm, clear, and confident.

As a woman leader, you must prioritize sleep because it restores your mind, regulates your emotions, and equips you to show up

Hydration and Clarity for a Better You
When you're not drinking enough water, your brain feels it first. Dehydration shows up as fatigue, headaches, lack of focus, and irritability, things that make it hard to lead yourself, let alone anyone else. I've learned that keeping a bottle of water with me throughout the day is one of the simplest ways to stay clear and focused. Hydration keeps your energy steady and your mind sharp, so you can lead with strength and resilience.

Lessons Learned
Thriving in every season doesn't mean doing it alone. Resilient leadership requires you to seek help early, prioritize your well-being, and build habits that fuel both your body and your mind. When you create rhythms of nourishment, rest, and renewal, you give yourself the energy and clarity to

lead through any challenge or environment with strength and confidence

Strategies for creating sustainable habits for peak performance

1. **Fuel with intention.** Pay close attention to what you're feeding your body and your mind. Every meal, every thought, and every habit either adds to your resilience or drains it.

2. **Eat for brain power.** Choose foods that boost focus, clarity, and performance. Fueling your brain with the right nutrients gives you the edge to make sound decisions, stay calm under stress, and execute with excellence.

3. **Decide on your energy.** Start each day by deciding how you want to feel, how you want to show up, and how you want to lead. Your energy is your choice; set the tone before others set it for you.

Your brain is the command center of your leadership. It consumes about 20% of your body's total energy (Shonte' Jovan Taylor, Optimind Institute), which means what you put in your body directly impacts how you think, decide, and lead. When you choose habits that fuel resilience, you are choosing to lead with clarity, energy, and strength, not just for your team and business, but for yourself.

Chapter 9 Reflective Activity:
Fueling Your Resilience

Take a moment to reflect on your current lifestyle habits for life, career and business. Which ones are fueling your resilience, and which ones are draining it?

Now, choose **one new habit** you can commit to for a week that will strengthen your resilience, whether it's adding a 10-minute movement break, journaling at night, drinking more water, or going to bed 30 minutes earlier.

Pay attention to how this habit shifts your clarity, focus, and energy. By tracking your consistency over the next 7 days, you'll see that small choices create lasting change—and those choices fuel you to lead with strength and confidence.

"Movement isn't just exercise; it's resilience in action."

Chapter 10: The Power of Movement and Brain Performance

Incorporating Movement to Enhance Your Resilience and Productivity

The power of movement! As you navigate life, career, and business, you're exposed to constant stress from your environment. Movement- physical activity in any form- is essential for your mental, physical, and emotional well-being. I know you're busy, but deciding not to move is a harmful choice. It doesn't have to be complicated, you can walk, dance, run, or exercise in ways that fit your lifestyle. Movement shifts your energy, restores your mental focus, and strengthens your resilience.

When you're under chronic stress, your brain and body are directly impacted, especially your hippocampus- your memory bank. If you find yourself forgetting small things, like where you left your keys, it's not always just "getting older." Stress overload affects both short- and long-term memory. That's why consistent movement matters. Moving your body helps release serotonin and increase dopamine, boosting your mood while reducing stress, anxiety, and depression. Over time, consistent movement fuels your brain to perform at a higher level, helping you navigate life, career, and business with more clarity and confidence.

Brain Performance from Movement

The impact of physical activity on brain health and emotional resilience is undeniable. Movement equips you to overcome challenges more easily because it builds a resilient mind. I know this personally because running became my anchor when I struggled with anxiety. Running was my go-to whenever the chatter in my head got louder. It gave me mental clarity, calmed my thoughts, and reminded me that I could push through anything. Running settled my mind when intrusive thoughts tried to take over. It helped me think clearly, make better decisions, stay present with my family, and show up with confidence. That's the power of movement, it transforms not just your body, but your mind.

Building New Habits for Sustainability

Building a routine that supports both mental and physical resilience starts with a decision: to move. Decide today when you'll begin, how much time you'll commit, and what type of activity you'll do. It doesn't have to be long or intense, it just has to be consistent. Whether you choose a walk around your neighborhood, a dance break in your living room, or a workout at the gym, the key is to keep it doable. Movement should not add stress; it should relieve it. Every step you take toward making movement a habit is a step toward becoming a stronger, more resilient you, for yourself, your family, and your team.

Boost Cognitive Function and Reduce Stress
The Three Simple Movements

Here are three simple routines you can incorporate into your busy day as a woman leader. These don't require hours in the gym or fancy equipment, just you, your commitment, and a few minutes of intentional movement.

1. **Push-Ups**

    You can do push-ups on the wall, on the ground, with full body up, or with your knees bent. Start small with three sets of 5, 10, or 15 reps to build consistency. Push-ups work your entire body, but they also train your mind to push through resistance. Every rep is a reminder that you're stronger than you think, and that strength builds your mental resilience as much as your physical.

2. **Wall Sits**

    This exercise can be done anywhere, at home, in your

office, or even in a hallway. Stand with your back against the wall, slide down into a chair position, and hold. You can extend your arms forward to add challenge. Set a timer for 20–30 seconds (or longer as you grow stronger) and repeat for three sets, three times a week. Wall sits build lower-body strength, but more importantly, they train your patience and focus. The burn you feel in your legs becomes a lesson in holding steady under pressure, the same way you do as a leader.

3. **Squats**

    Squats are another powerful, simple movement to add to your schedule. Start with bodyweight squats, then add arm raises for a full-body boost. As you progress, incorporate light weights (3–5 lbs.) for 10, 15, or 20 reps, repeating for three sets. Squats strengthen your lower body and core, but they also energize your mindset. With every rep, you remind yourself that growth comes from repetition and consistency.

These simple movements are part of the same practices I share in the *30-Day Holistic Guide,* where you'll also find other activities to help you track your consistency. Even with a busy schedule, no excuses. When you move regularly, you reduce stress, build strength, and strengthen your resilient mindset so you can lead without losing yourself while leading through life, career, and business.

Storytime: Moving Through Stress
When life is happening for me, when I feel the overwhelm of being a mom, managing my home, and running my business, I know that movement is what gets me out of that funk. It helps me keep going. It helps me gain the strength, clarity, and resilience I need to keep showing up for myself, my family, and my business.

During my 22-plus years of military service, I worked in many different environments. Some were high-stress; so high that bombs were being dropped, and I had to seek cover, not knowing the outcome would be. In those moments, movement was key to my safety. But movement wasn't just about survival it was what kept me mentally resilient. It reminded me that even in the most intense and uncertain environments, I could still move forward, stay grounded, and keep going.

Lessons Learned

Movement is more than exercise; it's fuel for your mind. When you create intentional movement in your daily life- no matter the season- you sharpen your thinking, expand your capacity, and build the resilience to keep leading forward.

Strategies for better brain performance

1. **Move with purpose.**

    Choose to add movement into your day, even in the small moments. A walk during lunch, a stretch between meetings, or a quick dance break can sustain your resilience and reset your energy.

2. **Boost your memory bank.**

    Movement activates parts of your brain that improve memory, focus, and creativity. It's not just about fitness; it's about strengthening your mind so you can process, decide, and lead with clarity.

3. **Build sustainable habits.**

    Find ways to move that fit your lifestyle. Whether it's running, yoga, strength training, or simply walking the neighborhood, consistency matters more than intensity. Sustainable movement is what keeps you resilient for the long haul.

Your body was built to move, and your mind was built to grow stronger because of it. Don't wait for stress to take over before you act. Every step, every stretch, and every intentional breath of movement is an investment in your resilience as a leader.

Chapter 10 Reflective Activity: Movement = Resilience in Action

Think about how movement has shown up in your life. How has moving your body- whether through walking, dancing, running, or exercising- shifted your energy, strengthened your focus, or helped you push through a challenge? Take a few minutes to answer the questions below:

1. When was the last time movement helped you reset your mind or emotions during a stressful moment?

2. What form of movement feels most natural and sustainable for you right now (walks, stretching, push-ups, dancing, running, etc.)?

3. How does your body and brain feel after you engage in movement, even for just 5–10 minutes?

4. What is one small movement habit you can commit to adding to your daily routine this week to boost your resilience and brain performance?

5. How will making this one movement choice daily impact your ability to lead in life, career, and business?

Movement isn't just exercise; it's resilience in action. Every time you choose to move, you choose clarity, strength, and leadership from a grounded place.

"Thriving in every season is not about perfection it's about presence, resilience, and choosing not to lose yourself along the way."

Chapter 11: Leading in Every Season- Self-Care as a Leadership Strategy to Lead in Any Season of Life, Career, and Business

Redefining Self-Care as an Essential Leadership Tool

You put a lot of time into your business, your family, and everything else. But if we're being honest, self-care is usually the last thing on your priority list. You say it has to get done, but it hasn't been your focus because you're so bogged down with life, career, business, and everything in between.

Now is the time to shift. As you step into becoming a resilient woman leader, you must not only know, but also believe that self-care is the key puzzle piece that keeps you grounded through the chaos of life, career, and business. At the end of the day, you want work and life alignment, and that alignment starts with you making yourself a priority. That means choosing your well-being every chance and every opportunity you get.

Maintaining Work-Life Integration

Maintaining work-life integration can be challenging if you don't put things in place. When you set boundaries to protect your time, energy, and well-being, you thrive. But too often you say "yes" to things you should be saying "no" to.

You have to assess your time and know exactly where it's going, because when you know your time, you can create space for wellness and self-care. Being a resilient woman leader is about optimizing your time and your overall well-being.

Your well-being is a 360 holistic approach, including physical activity, mindset, nutrition, and sleep. And let's pause here: the amount of sleep you're getting each night is critical. Quality sleep impacts your brain function and performance. Every night as you sleep, your brain filters out and discards unwanted, toxic cells and regenerates itself. Think of it as your brain decluttering every night. But if you're not getting quality sleep, your brain can't do its job. Quality sleep is a must.

Storytime: Putting Myself First: A Self-Care Journey
As I continue to build my business and my life at this young age of forty-plus, I have made my well-being my top priority. Why? Because I've experienced burnout, extreme stress,

divorce, and the death of a parent, so I understand the toll trauma in all forms brings on us mentally, emotionally, and physically.

Today, and for many days to come, I choose to put myself first. For me, that looks like moving my body five times a week, getting monthly massages, taking solo trips, and enjoying solo dates. I've learned to enjoy life without guilt. I put myself first so I can be there for my children, show up whole in my business, and thrive.

These practices have allowed me to continue building a resilient mindset and to keep operating as a resilient woman leader, especially now as I've transitioned into being a full-time business owner after serving 22+ years in the United States Air Force.

So, my friend, this is your reminder: always put your well-being first. When you do, you'll be able to build the business, life, and career you truly desire, without losing yourself in the process.

Lessons Learned:

Choose yourself first to live the life you desire and thrive in every season of life, career, and business. When you do, you stop running on empty and start leading from a place of strength, clarity, and wholeness.

Self-Reflection Activity:

Take this time to answer these questions and trust yourself to do the things that you have been stopping yourself from doing. That can give you the reset you need to start thriving in life, career, and business.

What have you been wanting to do, but haven't given yourself permission to start?

What is one self-care practice you will commit to for the next three to six months?

How will you remind yourself daily that putting your well-being first makes you stronger for everyone else?

Strategies for thriving in every season

Prioritize restoration.
Commit to at least one monthly self-care practice, whether it's a massage, a solo date, or a quiet day off, that recharges your energy and restores your balance.

Protect your presence.
Be intentional about limiting the work you bring home.

Create boundaries so you can show up fully present with the people who matter most.

Anchor your seasons.

Recognize the season you're in, whether it's a season of stretching, slowing down, or rebuilding, and give yourself permission to lead differently in each one.

Every season will demand something different from you. Some seasons will stretch you, others will slow you down, but all of them can grow you. When you choose yourself first, you give yourself the strength to lead through it all, with clarity, resilience, and purpose.

"Purpose isn't found in the perfect moments; it's built in the messy ones. When you operate with clarity, intention, and grace, you stop chasing and start leading."

Closing

Woman, Breathe: Leading Through Life, Career, and Business While Thriving in Every Season.
Integrating the Principles of Resilient Leadership into Daily Life

Woman, Breathe: Leading Through Life, Career, and Business While Thriving in Every Season is not something you just read and put down; it's a guide you can live by. These principles are strategies you can apply daily to lead through your life, career, and business no matter the season you find yourself in.

It's not about sporadic habits. It's about consistent daily actions, even if they're just 5 or 10 minutes. Those simple choices shift your mindset, build and sustain your resilience, and help you overcome the challenges you encounter in your life, career, and business.

And the beautiful part? Continuing to apply these practices doesn't just impact you, it impacts the people around you. When you choose to become a resilient woman leader, the quality of your life shifts, and the ripple effect touches your family, your team, and your community.

Your ability to lead well in any role impacts the culture of your work or business. It impacts your people. It equips them to become more resilient, to make sound decisions, to handle stressful situations, to communicate more effectively, and to show greater empathy.

Thriving in every season is the cornerstone of creating the life, career, and business you've dreamed of. *Woman, Breathe* is your reminder to create the space to breathe, knowing you've done the work. You've built the mental resilience to face what's in front of you and lead through it with strength.

As you continue your journey through life, career, and business, I want you to remember this: I'm proof that resilience can be built, and now, so are you.

Chapter Summary: Thriving in Every Season

Here's a summary of the concepts shared in this book to help you lead and thrive in every season of life, career, and business:

- **Chapter 1: Mindset Identity**
  You discovered how your mindset and identity are the driving forces that allow you to lead and thrive in every season of life, career, and business.

- **Chapter 2: Managing Your Emotions**
  You learned how to manage your emotions and remain resilient through chaos while growing in self-awareness and self-management.

- **Chapter 3: The Resilient Leader Mindset**
  Taking control of your thoughts allows you to take back control of your life, career, and business, and to operate in a growth mindset no matter the season you're in.

- **Chapter 4: Effective Decision-Making: A Defining Element of Leadership**
  When you choose yourself first, you unlock the

courage to lead and the power to thrive in every season of life, career, and business.

- **Chapter 5: Stress Management for Leading with Resilience**

    Managing stress is not optional; it's essential. You now have strategies and tools to prevent burnout and lead with resilience in every season.

- **Chapter 6: Building & Leading Resilient Teams**

    By trusting yourself and leading with confidence, you gain the strength and resilience to guide your team through change and uncertainty

- **Chapter 7: Leading Through Communication and Managing Conflict**

    How you communicate can either build or destroy resilience, trust, culture, and growth. You've seen that your tone and approach shape how your team responds, how conflict is resolved, and how you lead through pressure.

- **Chapter 8: Operating With Purpose**

    Operating in your purpose requires clarity, intention, and grace. By returning to your *why*, leaning on your strengths, and releasing limits, you create a business and life rooted in sustainability and impact.

- **Chapter 9: Lifestyle Habits for Resilient Leadership**
  Thriving in every season requires more than hard work; it requires fueling your body and mind. You learned that what you eat, how you rest, and the habits you build directly shape your energy, clarity, and resilience.

- **Chapter 10: The Power of Movement and Brain Performance**
  Movement is more than exercise; it's fuel for your brain. By creating intentional daily movement, you sharpen your thinking, reduce stress, and build the mental resilience to lead confidently through any season.

- **Chapter 11: Leading in Every Season**
  Self-care is not selfish; it's a leadership strategy. When you choose yourself first, set boundaries, and practice restoration, you create the strength to thrive in every season of life, career, and business.

About the Author
Who Is Shevon?

The woman and friend many know as *Shevvy*.

I was born in Bagotstown, Guyana, South America, in the '90s, to loving and hard-working parents. I come from very humble beginnings and a loving family. I grew up in a one-bedroom home with ten family members, on a street lined with tropical fruit trees—mangoes, papayas, genips, bananas, and more. My childhood was filled with simple joys: playing barefoot after school, chasing chickens in the yard, and walking with my siblings to school or to the market for fresh vegetables.

We didn't have running water; sometimes we carried water from the well. We didn't always have electricity at night; we used lanterns. Even though we lacked material things, our home was full of love. Looking back, I see now that resilience was built into my family, my culture, and into me.

As my journey took me from Guyana to the United States, to serving 22+ years in the United States. Air Force, to now becoming Founder and CEO of MAC Leadership Academy and J3M Consulting. I have lived through challenges and victories. I've experienced career fulfillment and setbacks.

Divorce. Betrayal. The loss of a parent. The loss of friendships I thought would last a lifetime. I've battled anxiety and fear. But through it all, I discovered the true meaning of resilience.

Breaking through my mental barriers allowed me to dig deep, push through fear, and build the life, career, and business I desired. Every day, I continue to strengthen my resilient mindset. Because challenges never stop coming, but resilience equips me to face them with steadiness and strength.

Today, I live by this truth: resilience is built within. And just as it was built in me, it will be built in you.

As you read this book, I invite you to reflect on your own journey: where you've been, where you're going, and the life you want to create. Identify the things weighing on your mind, causing stress, worry, or fatigue. And know this: you have the resilience to navigate life, career, and business without losing yourself in the process.

Additional Information

The Journey Continues

My commitment to resilience and thriving in every season and my hopes for you.

You've walked through the pages with me. You've reflected, practiced, and started building habits that fuel your mind, body, and leadership. Life will keep life-ing, but now you have the tools to lead yourself, your family, your team, and your business with clarity and courage.

If you've finished this book and you're thinking, "I want support to actually do this every day," don't worry, I've created a mentorship experience for you.

Your Next Steps

Work with Shevvy
Access Free Resources and Digital Products:

www.womanbreathe.com

Woman, Breathe™: Reset, Lead & Thrive Intensive: a five-day guided experience to help you reset your mind, lead with clarity, and thrive in your next season.

Thriving in Every Season Mentorship Program: **Who this is for**

Ambitious, purpose-driven women who want to lead with strength and thrive in every season of life, career, and business.

What we focus on

1. Self-awareness. Strength. Stewardship. Sustainability.
2. Managing stress and emotions. Decision-making. Communication and conflict.
3. Purpose, and Habits.
4. Turning the principles in this book into daily action.

The promise

We will keep it practical. We will keep it personal. We will keep you moving forward.

How to get started

I. Join the Woman, Breathe Slack community

Use the QR code title **Woman, Breath Slack Community**.

1. Scan the Woman, Breathe **Slack Community** QR code.
2. Enter your email to receive your invite.

3. Open the Slack invite and click **Join**.

4. Set your display name so we know it's you.

5. In the **#introductions** channel, share your name, city, and the chapter that hit home for you.

II. Choose the path that fits you best. Follow the steps exactly so nothing gets missed.

1. Book a call by scanning the QR code titled **Book a Call with your phone** on this page.

2. Select a date that fits your schedule and choose a time.

3. Complete the Thrive in Every Season Mentorship Interest call form.

4. Tap Confirm. Check your email for the calendar invite and meeting link.

Alternate: visit macleadershipacademy.com and click Book a Call.

III. Bring me into your organization

If you are an organizational leader and want keynotes, workshops, or leadership development for your women leaders:

1. Email us at info@macleadershipacademy.com
2. In the email please include: your organization name, type of support you're requesting, (speaking, training, executive coaching), desired date range, audience size, goals for the session, preferred format (virtual or in-person), and budget range.
3. You will receive a message and next steps after your email is received.

IV. Connect with me on LinkedIn

Scan the QR code titled **SCAN ME** to connect with me on LinkedIn.

1. Tap **Connect**.
2. Add a note that says: "I just finished *Woman, Breathe*. Here's my biggest takeaway: _____."
3. I read these personally so expect a message from me.

References

American Heart Association. (2023). *Women and stress.* https://www.heart.org/en/healthy-living/healthy-lifestyle/stress-management/women-and-stress

Bradberry, T., & Greaves, J. (2009). *Emotional intelligence 2.0.* TalentSmart.

Dweck, C. S. (2006). *Mindset: The new psychology of success.* Random House.

Keller, A., Litzelman, K., Wisk, L. E., Maddox, T., Cheng, E. R., Creswell, P. D., & Witt, W. P. (2012). Does the perception that stress affects health matter? The association with health and mortality. *Health Psychology, 31*(5), 677–684. https://doi.org/10.1037/a0026743

McKinsey & Company. (2023). *Women in the workplace.* https://www.mckinsey.com/featured-insights/diversity-and-inclusion/women-in-the-workplace

Taylor, S. J. (n.d.). *Neuroscience 102: Neuroscience to manage emotions [Video 3: The neuroscience of emotions, stress, and memory].* The Optimind Institute.

U.S. Department of Health and Human Services, Office on

Women's Health. (2021). *Stress and your health.* https://womenshealth.gov/mental-health/good-mental-health/stress-and-your-health

www.ingramcontent.com/pod-product-compliance
Lightning Source LLC
Chambersburg PA
CBHW030901170426
43193CB00009BA/693